English In Tune

Robert Hickling | Shun Morimoto

NATIONAL
GEOGRAPHIC
LEARNING

Australia · Brazil · Mexico · Singapore · United Kingdom · United States

English In Tune

Robert Hickling / Shun Morimoto

© 2022 Cengage Learning K.K.

Photo Credits:

Cover: © Luciano Mortula | Dreamstime.com; 9: © stock.adobe.com; 10: © dpa/ 時事通信フォト ; 15: © stock.adobe.com; 16: © stock.adobe.com; 20: © shutterstock; 21: © stock.adobe.com; 22: © stock.adobe.com; 27: © stock.adobe.com; 28: © Zniehf | Dreamstime.com; 33: © stock.adobe.com; 34: © stock.adobe.com; 39: © stock.adobe.com; 40: © photolibrary; 45: © stock.adobe.com; 46: © stock.adobe.com; 51: © stock.adobe.com; 52: © stock.adobe.com; 55: © stock.adobe.com; 57: © stock.adobe.com; 58: © photolibrary; 63: © stock.adobe.com; 64: © stock.adobe.com; 69: © Kobby Dagan | Dreamstime.com; 70: © Shengying Lin | Dreamstime.com; 75 © stock.adobe.com; 76: © Hugoht | Dreamstime.com; 81: © Felix Mizioznikov- stock.adobe.com; 82: © stock.adobe.com; 87: ©stock.adobe.com; 88: © stock.adobe.com; 93: © NASA Image Library; 94: © 時事

For permission to use material from this textbook or product, e-mail to **eltjapan@cengage.com**

ISBN: 978-4-86312-393-9

National Geographic Learning | Cengage Learning K.K.
No. 2 Funato Building 5th Floor
1-11-11 Kudankita, Chiyoda-ku
Tokyo 102-0073
Japan

Tel: 03-3511-4392
Fax: 03-3511-4391

はしがき

　本書は、大学生が英語を通して情報や考えを理解し、表現することができるようになることを目的としたテキストです。書名に「調和した」という意味を表す in tune を冠することで、4 技能を有機的に統合し、総合的な英語運用能力を身に付けることができるようデザインされています。

　本書は計 15 の Unit から成り、各 Unit はテーマに関する **Warm-Up Questions**、**Reading**、**Listening**、**Speaking**、**Writing** の 5 つのセクションから構成されています。理解を主眼とした **Reading** と **Listening** の後に **Speaking** と **Writing** を通した表現活動を行うという学修の流れになっています。

　Warm-Up Questions では、テーマに関する簡単な問いに答えることによって既存の知識（スキーマ）を活性化し、学修に向けたレディネスを高めます。**Reading** では、スポーツや食、宇宙、偉人、スマートテクノロジー、SNS をはじめとした、大学生が高い興味・関心を示すトピックを取り上げています。セクションの冒頭には英文を読むにあたって有用なストラテジーを紹介していますので、それを意識して読むことによって、リーディング力の向上を図ることができます。文章を読んだ後に語彙や内容理解の問題を解き、正確に内容を理解できたかどうかを確認します。

　Listening では、英語を聞く際に知っておくと有用なポイントを学修します。リエゾン（連結）や同化、L の発音、子音の連続、弱形など、従来の教科書では比較的手薄であった英語の音声面を取り上げます。エクササイズは、会話の内容理解や提示された質問に対する適切な応答を選択する問題から構成されており、各種外部試験対策にも役立つはずです。

　Speaking では、「許可を求める」や「依頼を断る」といった言語の機能的な側面に着目した表現や、フィラーや相づち、Yes・No で答えられない時の返し方など、実際の会話ですぐに使える表現を数多く紹介しています。会話例を通してそれぞれの表現の使い方を理解した上で、会話文の作成や各種ペア活動を行います。

　最後の **Writing** では、「順序」や「目的」、「例示」といった表現をカテゴリー別に整理したり、物や人物の描写、概念説明、問題発見・解決型の文章の書き方などを学修したりします。例文を通してポイントを掴んだ後、アウトラインを作成して文章を書く活動を行います。

　以上の流れを通して、4 技能の総合的な運用力を高めることができる点が本書の特徴です。また、本書では英語に苦手意識をもっている学生にも取り組みやすくなるよう、解説や指示文を日本語で表記しました。

　本書を通して多くのみなさんが自信をもって英語を使い、英語によるコミュニケーションを楽しむことができるようになってもらえれば幸いです。

著者一同

Table of Contents

Unit	Title	Reading
1	Dreams and Aspirations	5W1H に着目して内容を読み取ろう **Reading Topic** *The Bucket List*
2	Sports and Leisure	比較・対照に着目して英文を読もう **Reading Topic** Esports
3	Routines and Habits	主語を正確に捉えて英文を読もう **Reading Topic** Pet Peeves
4	Social Behavior	パラグラフごとのメインアイデアを捉えよう **Reading Topic** Social Loafing
5	University Life	《列挙》の表現に着目して英文を読もう **Reading Topic** Online Learning
6	Culture and Traditions	《時》を表す表現に着目して流れをつかもう **Reading Topic** Manga
7	Four Seasons	未知語の意味を文脈から推測しながら読もう **Reading Topic** *Sakura*—Cherry Blossoms
8	Shopping Preferences	返り読みをしないよう意識して英文を読もう **Reading Topic** Social Media Influencers
9	Safety and Security	ビジュアル情報を活用して内容を理解しよう **Reading Topic** Nightingale Floors
10	Smart Technology	用語の定義を正確に捉えて読もう **Reading Topic** The Internet of Things
11	Celebrations and Festivals	英文を読む前に背景知識を活性化させよう **Reading Topic** American Independence Day
12	Taking Care of Our Environment	数値に着目して正確に内容を読み取ろう **Reading Topic** Our Carbon Footprint
13	Important People—Past and Present	指示語に着目して内容を読み取ろう **Reading Topic** Charles Darwin
14	Food and Health	修飾関係に注目して英文を読もう **Reading Topic** Superfoods
15	Space Exploration	意味のかたまり（チャンク）単位で内容を読み取ろう **Reading Topic** Hayabusa2

本書の構成と使い方

各 Unit は 6 ページ構成です。以下に、それぞれの項目やアクティビティの目的と使い方を説明します。

Warm-Up Questions

テーマに関する簡単な問いに答えます。学修に向け既存の知識を活性化し、レディネスを高めます。

Reading

テーマに関する 280 語ほどの英文を読みます。冒頭のストラテジーを意識して読むことで、読解力が向上します。

A Vocabulary Builder

本文を理解する上で重要な語句の意味を確認します。

B Comprehension Questions

本文の内容理解を確認する 3 択問題です。重要なポイントの理解を深めます。

C Paragraph Summaries

パラグラフの要約文を本文の構成に合わせて並べ替え、本文全体の理解を確認します。

Listening

英語を聞く際に知っておくと有用なポイントを学修します。

Task ▶ 連結や同化など英語の音声の特徴を取り上げ、聞き取る練習をします。

A **B** テーマに関する同じ会話を聞いて、内容理解とディクテーションを行います。

C 英語の質問を聞いて、適切な応答を選びます。

Speaking

英語の機能別の表現や実際の会話ですぐに使える表現を取り上げています。

Ex. ▶ 取り上げた表現が実際の会話でどのように使われているかを学修します。

A 実際に会話文を作成し、ペアで練習をします。

B テーマについて、ペアで会話練習をします。

Writing

英語表現をカテゴリー別に整理したり、英文の代表的な型を学修したりします。

Ex. ▶ 実際の英文で学修項目がどのように使われているかを学びます。

Task ▶ アウトラインを作成し、テーマに関する文章を書く練習をします。

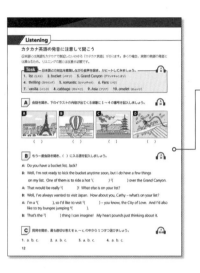

音声ファイルの利用方法

 のアイコンがある箇所の音声ファイルにアクセスできます。

https://ngljapan.com/eitune-audio/

❶ 上記の URL にアクセス、または QR コードをスマートフォンなどのリーダーでスキャン

❷ 表示されるファイル名をクリックして音声ファイルをダウンロードまたは再生

Dreams and Aspirations

みなさんには将来の夢や人生で成し遂げたいことはありますか。やりがいのある職業に就きたい、世界一周旅行をしたい、素敵なパートナーに出会いたいなど、人によってさまざまなものがあるはずです。この Unit では夢や希望について英語で理解したり表現したりする練習をしましょう。

Warm-Up Questions

次の質問に対して英語で答えましょう。

1. What were some of your hopes and dreams when you were a child?

   _____

   _____

2. What are three things you want to do before you die?

   _____

   _____

5W1H に着目して内容を読み取ろう

英文を読むときは、5W1H (When: いつ、Where: どこで、Who: 誰が、What: 何を、Why: なぜ、How: どのように) に着目し、場面ごとに状況を捉えることが大切です。

The Bucket List

[1]　*The Bucket List* is a 2007 American movie about billionaire Edward Cole (Jack Nicholson) and blue-collar car mechanic Carter Chambers (Morgan Freeman), both
5▸ of whom suffer from terminal lung cancer. The two elderly men end up having to share the same hospital room where they are being treated. Despite having very different backgrounds and personalities, Edward and Carter eventually become friends.

[2]　While in the hospital, Carter starts writing a bucket list—a list of things he'd like
10▸ to do before he dies, or "kicks the bucket." However, after hearing that he has less than one year to live, he dejectedly throws it away. The next morning, Edward finds the discarded list and encourages Carter to do everything on it. He adds a few items of his own, and offers to cover all costs.

[3]　Against his wife's objections, Carter accepts Edward's offer. The two men then set
15▸ out on an incredible journey, one that includes skydiving, flying over the North Pole, a visit to the Taj Mahal, riding motorcycles on the Great Wall of China, and a lion safari in Tanzania.

[4]　After they return, Carter collapses and is rushed to the hospital. The cancer has spread to his brain. He undergoes surgery, but dies on the operating table. Edward
20▸ delivers a eulogy at Carter's funeral, explaining that the last three months of Carter's life were the best three months of his own life. Before Edward dies, he reunites with his estranged daughter, who introduces him to the granddaughter he never knew he had. After kissing the girl on the cheek, Edward carefully crosses "Kiss the most beautiful girl in the world" off his bucket list.

Words: terminal lung cancer 末期の肺癌　eventually ついに　discarded 捨てられた　surgery 手術　eulogy 賛辞　estranged 疎遠になった　cross ... off （リストから）…を消す

A Vocabulary Builder

次の単語の本文中での意味を、a. 〜 c. の中から１つずつ選びましょう。

1. mechanic (line 3):   a. salesperson   b. repairperson   c. designer

2. dejectedly (line 11):   a. disappointedly   b. quickly   c. angrily

3. cover (line 13):   a. pay for   b. count   c. hide

4. collapses (line 18):   a. feels tired   b. becomes sick   c. falls down

B Comprehension Questions

完成した英文が本文の内容に合うように、a. 〜 c. の中から最も適切なものを１つずつ選びましょう。

1. Edward and Carter (a. have similar personalities   b. come from the same background
   c. have the same illness).

2. Carter throws away his bucket list when (a. he learns that he will die within a year
   b. Edward sees it   c. Edward tells him that it's silly to write one).

3. Carter accepts Edward's offer (a. after promising his wife that he will be careful
   b. despite his wife's protests   c. at the encouragement of his wife).

4. One item on Edward's bucket list was (a. to meet his granddaughter for the first time
   b. to kiss the most beautiful girl in the world   c. to kiss his daughter).

C Paragraph Summaries

次の英文が表している本文の段落番号を（　）に記入しましょう。

(　) Carter accepts Edward's offer, and they soon begin the trip of a lifetime.

(　) *The Bucket List* is a movie about two elderly men, Edward and Carter, who first meet in the hospital where they are being treated for terminal cancer.

(　) Soon after returning from their trip, Carter dies. Edward decides to visit his estranged daughter and, to his joy, learns that he has a granddaughter.

(　) One day Edward finds Carter's discarded bucket list, adds his own items to it, and suggests that they live out their bucket lists together at his expense.

Listening

カタカナ英語の発音に注意して聞こう

日本語には英語をカタカナで表記したいわゆる「カタカナ英語」があります。多くの場合、実際の英語の発音とは異なるため、リスニングの際には注意が必要です。

Task — 日本語との対比を意識しながら音声を聞き、リピートしてみましょう。

1. list（リスト） 2. bucket（バケツ） 3. Grand Canyon（グランドキャニオン）

4. thrilling（スリリング） 5. romantic（ロマンチック） 6. Paris（パリ）

7. vanilla（バニラ） 8. cabbage（キャベツ） 9. Asia（アジア） 10. omelet（オムレツ）

A 会話を聞き、下のイラストの内容が出てくる順番に 1 ～ 4 の番号を（ ）に記入しましょう。

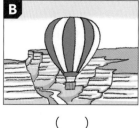

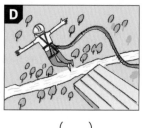

（　　）　　　　　（　　）　　　　　（　　）　　　　　（　　）

B もう一度会話を聞き、（ ）に単語を記入しましょう。

A: Do you have a bucket list, Jack?

B: Well, I'm not ready to kick the bucket anytime soon, but I *do* have a few things

  on my list. One of them is to ride a hot ¹(   ) ²(   ) over the Grand Canyon.

A: That would be really ³(   )! What else is on your list?

B: Well, I've always wanted to visit Japan. How about you, Cathy – what's on your list?

A: I'm a ⁴(   ), so I'd like to visit ⁵(   ) – you know, the City of Love. And I'd also
  like to try bungee jumping ⁶(   ).

B: That's the ⁷(   ) thing I can imagine! My heart pounds just thinking about it.

C 質問を聞き、最も適切な答えを a. ～ c. の中から 1 つずつ選びましょう。

1. a. b. c.　　　　2. a. b. c.　　　　3. a. b. c.　　　　4. a. b. c.

Speaking

《自分がしたいこと》を表す表現を使って会話をしよう

自分がしたいことを伝える際、want to … や would like to … といった表現を使うことが多いですが、英語にはその他にもさまざまな表現があります。ニュアンスや場面に応じて使えるように練習しましょう。

> Let me *do* … 「…させてください」、I feel like *doing* … 「…したい気分です」、I'd rather *do* … 「むしろ…したいです」

Ex.

1. A: Are you free this afternoon? Let's go to the movies.

   B: Umm … I'm a bit tired, so **I'd rather stay home**.

2. A: What do you want to eat for dinner?

   B: I had spaghetti last night, so **I feel like having Japanese food**.

3. A: **Let me carry your suitcase**, grandma.

   B: Oh, thank you. That's very kind of you.

A 上で挙げた表現を 2 つ使って次の会話を完成させましょう。完成後、パートナーと練習しましょう。

A: Where would you like to go someday?

B: I _____.

A: Oh, really? Why do you want to go there?

B: I want to _____ and _____.

A: That sounds _____. When do you think you'll go?

B: Well, _____.

B 次の内容について、パートナーと会話をしましょう。

*genie ジーニー (ランプの精)

1. Before I graduate, I'd like to _____.

2. In the future, I don't want to live in _____. I'd rather live in _____.

3. I don't feel like _____ now, but I may when I'm older.

4. If a genie* gave me one wish, I would say, "Please let me _____."

Writing

《理由》を表す表現を使って英文を書こう

自分の意見や主張を述べる際、理由を加えることによって説得力が増します。英語には理由を表すさまざまな表現があり、以下はその一例です。意識的に使ってレパートリーを広げましょう。

> **because [since / as] S+V** S が V だから　**for this reason** この理由で　**one of the reasons is (because/ that) S+V** 主な理由の 1 つは S が V だからです　**this [that] is why S+V** こう（そう）いう理由で S が V です　**the reason why S+V is …** S が V なのは…だからです

Ex.

I would like to be a high school teacher after I graduate from university. **One of the reasons is because** my mother is an elementary school teacher. She often tells me how fulfilling her work is. **Another reason is that** I love English. I started teaching English at a tutoring school, and I'm really enjoying it. I want students to know that being able to use English will broaden their view of the world. **For these reasons**, my dream is to become a high school English teacher.

POINT それぞれの理由に対して実際の経験などの具体的な情報を補うと説得力が増します。

Task ▶大学卒業後に就きたい職業についてのパラグラフを書きましょう。

Step 1 以下のフレームを使ってアウトラインを作りましょう。

A job I would like to have: _____

Reason 1: _____

    Extra information: _____

Reason 2: _____

    Extra information: _____

Step 2 Step 1 のアウトラインをもとにパラグラフを書きましょう。

After I graduate from university, I would like to _____.

One reason is _____

_____.

_____

_____.

Unit 2

Sports and Leisure

スポーツやレジャー（余暇の活動）は、私たちを日々の慌ただしい生活から解放し、心と身体をリフレッシュさせてくれます。ワークライフバランスが叫ばれる今日、その重要性はますます高まっています。この Unit では、スポーツやレジャーについて英語で理解したり表現したりする練習をしましょう。

Warm-Up Questions

次のイラストが何のスポーツを表しているかを英語で答えましょう。

1.

_____

2.

_____

3.

_____

4.

_____

5.

_____

6.

_____

7.

_____

8.

_____

Reading

比較・対照に着目して英文を読もう

英語の文章には、2 つの物事を比較・対照させながらそれぞれの特徴や相違点を説明するタイプのものがあります。どのような観点からの比較が行われているのかを捉えた上で、詳細な説明を読み取りましょう。

Esports

① Esports is a general term to describe video game competitions typically played by professional gamers. Much like traditional sporting events like soccer, baseball, golf and so on, esports games are often played
5▶ before live audiences or broadcast over the Internet. Esports has grown to become a billion-dollar industry, with a viewership of about 500 million people a year worldwide.

② An esports game is performed in much the same way as a traditional sport, with clear rules and penalties handed out by a referee if any of the rules are broken. In addition, sportscasters are usually there to provide live descriptions of the game. Full-
10▶ time professional video game players, or pro gamers, regularly compete for cash prizes in professional tournaments. These tournaments are usually sponsored by technology companies, with other revenue coming through live ticket sales and online viewing subscriptions.

③ While traditional sports require players to compete against each other in a physical
15▶ location and to exert more physical effort while playing, esports does not necessarily require the physical presence of players—all they need is an Internet connection. This is the biggest difference between the two activities. A second major difference is the games themselves. Although traditional sports may see minor rule changes from time to time, the fundamental rules remain the same. On the other hand, in competitive gaming,
20▶ both minor and major updates to games are frequently made, forcing gamers to adapt quickly and to develop new strategies.

④ Opinion seems to be divided as to whether or not esports should be considered real sports. There is no denying, however, that esports is a booming global industry where skilled players fiercely compete against each other and attract large numbers of fans.

Words: broadcast 放送される　viewership 視聴者層　referee 審判　sportscasters スポーツ解説者
subscriptions サブスクリプション（定額視聴）　no denying 否定できない　fiercely 熾烈に

A Vocabulary Builder

次の単語の本文中での意味を、a.〜c.の中から1つずつ選びましょう。

1. sponsored (line 11):　　a. attended　　b. played　　c. promoted

2. revenue (line 12):　　a. interest　　b. money　　c. tax

3. exert (line 15):　　a. apply　　b. demand　　c. develop

4. adapt (line 20):　　a. accept　　b. approve　　c. adjust

B Comprehension Questions

完成した英文が本文の内容に合うように、a.〜c.の中から最も適切なものを1つずつ選びましょう。

1. Esports has a worldwide audience of around (**a.** 5,000,000　**b.** 50,000,000
   c. 500,000,000) people a year.

2. Full-time esports gamers are called (**a.** game pros　**b.** pro gamers　**c.** esport pros).

3. Esports gamers often have to devise new game plans to (**a.** solve old problems　**b.**
   reach the next level　**c.** keep up with game updates).

4. The passage concludes by pointing out (**a.** two similarities　**b.** two differences　**c.** one
   similarity and one difference) between esports and traditional sports.

C Paragraph Summaries

次の英文が表している本文の段落番号を（　）に記入しましょう。

(　) Despite similarities between esports and traditional sports, there is debate about
   whether or not esports should fall under the category of "sport."

(　) There are several major differences between esports and physical sports.

(　) Esports and athletic sports are both often played in front of live crowds or viewed on
   the Internet.

(　) Like professional sports, esports has game officials, sportscasters, sponsors and cash
   prizes.

Listening

イントネーションを意識して聞こう

英語の文は、主に上昇調と下降調のイントネーションで発音されます。平叙文と WH 疑問文、命令文は下降調、YES-NO 疑問文は上昇調となるのが基本的なルールです。

Task イントネーションを意識して英文を聞き、リピートしましょう。

1. Are you free this weekend? (↗)
2. I used to live in Tokyo. (↘)
3. Raise your hand. (↘)
4. What would you like? (↘)
5. Did you go shopping yesterday? (↗)
6. How's the weather today? (↘)

A 会話を聞き、下のイラストの内容が出てくる順番に 1 〜 4 の番号を（ ）に記入しましょう。

( )   ( )   ( )   ( )

B もう一度会話を聞き、（ ）に単語を記入しましょう。

A: Are you ¹( ) sports or fitness, Bob?

B: Yeah, I played basketball in junior and senior high school. It was a lot of fun, but I wasn't very good at it. Now I belong to a fitness club. I ²( ) ³( ) two or three times a week. How about you, Carol?

A: Well, I play badminton once in a ⁴( ). … Oh, and I like bowling, too, but I guess that's not ⁵( ) a sport, is it?

B: No, not really. … Hey, what's your best ⁶( )?

A: ⁷( ) me see … 42, I think.

C 質問を聞き、最も適切な答えを a. 〜 c. の中から 1 つずつ選びましょう。

1. a. b. c.   2. a. b. c.   3. a. b. c.   4. a. b. c.

Speaking

《禁止》 の表現を使って会話をしよう

日常会話では、「〜してはいけない」 という 《禁止》 を表すことがあります。 以下はその代表的な表現です。

S must not [cannot] *do* ... 、S be not allowed to *do* ... 、Don't [Never] *do* ... 、S be not supposed to *do* ... 、Please refrain from *doing* ... 、*Doing* is prohibited

Ex.

A: How is wheelchair basketball different from regular basketball?

B: Well, in regular basketball, players **are not allowed** to hold the ball while dribbling, but it's permitted in wheelchair basketball. And in wheelchair basketball, players **cannot** lift from their chairs. They must remain firmly seated at all times.

A: Sounds interesting. I'd like to watch a game sometime.

A 《禁止》 の表現を 2 つ使って次の会話を完成させましょう。 完成後、 ペアで練習しましょう。

A: What's a difficult sport or game for you to play?

B: For me, _____.

A: Oh, really? What makes it difficult?

B: Well, _____.

A: I see. And can you give me another reason?

B: _____.

B 次の質問についてパートナーと会話をしましょう。

What are three things you like to do in your free time? How much time do you spend doing them each week?

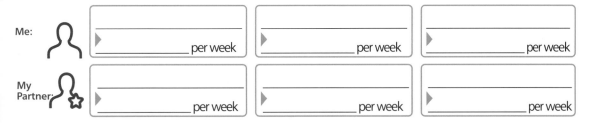

Writing

写真やイラストを描写する英文を書こう

写真やイラストなどを説明する英文を書くときは、《全体》から《細部》という流れで構成すると良いでしょう。まずは場所がどこなのか、誰がいる（何がある）のか、時間はいつなのかといった全体的な情報を提示します。そしてそれぞれの人物や物事についての具体的な詳細情報を述べます。

Ex.

〔全体〕There are six people in the picture, three men and three women. They all look fairly young. They are working out in the gym. 〔細部〕Two people are running on treadmills*, and three people are doing weight-lifting. One woman is drinking water and taking a rest.

*treadmill ランニングマシーン

Task 以下のイラストを説明するパラグラフを書きましょう。

Step 1 イラストを見て、説明に必要となる語句を調べましょう。

Words and Phrases

General description of the picture

- *park*
- *4 people*
-
-

Details

-
-
-
-

Step 2 Step 1のアウトラインをもとにパラグラフを書きましょう。

_____

_____

_____

_____

Unit 3

Routines and Habits

毎朝起きたら歯を磨いたり、寝る前にストレッチをしたりするなど、私たちには意識する、しないに関わらず、日々繰り返し行う行動（ルーティーン）があります。この Unit では、私たちが日常的に行うことや習慣について英語で理解したり表現したりする練習をしましょう。

Warm-Up Questions

以下の活動を普段の生活でどの程度行いますか。当てはまる頻度に✓を入れましょう。

How often do you ...?

	never 決して〜しない	hardly ever ほとんど〜しない	sometimes 時々〜する	often よく〜する
1. cook	☐	☐	☐	☐
2. go to karaoke	☐	☐	☐	☐
3. oversleep	☐	☐	☐	☐
4. study	☐	☐	☐	☐
5. read books	☐	☐	☐	☐
6. do exercise	☐	☐	☐	☐
7. watch TV	☐	☐	☐	☐

主語を正確に捉えて英文を読もう

英文の骨格は、《S（主語）＋V（動詞）（＋α）》であり、主語を正確に捉えることが重要です。英語では関係代名詞や前置詞を伴った長い主語や、無生物主語が主語に来る場合があるので注意が必要です。

Pet Peeves

① As humans, we all have pet peeves—things that we find annoying, like slow drivers or talking during a movie—or disgusting, like loud chewing or cleaning
5 ▸ your ears in public. In most cases, a person's pet peeve may hardly be noticed by others. There are, however, some annoyances that
are almost universal, and require a bit of scientific research in order to understand why.

② One of the oldest and most common pet peeves is the sound of fingernails scratching
10 ▸ a chalkboard. The unpleasant sound actually causes a very measurable physical reaction. There is also a psychological aspect involved. In one study, listeners who knew that the sound was that of fingernails on a chalkboard rated it as more unpleasant than when they thought the sound came from a musical composition. In both cases, however, the physical part of the response remained the same. Other studies suggest
15 ▸ that the shape of our ear canals is responsible for the unpleasant feeling, as they seem to amplify certain high frequency sounds, thereby causing a certain amount of discomfort.

③ Another very common pet peeve is a dislike for slimy food. Many people have a natural distrust, or even a disgust, for foods that have an odd, slimy texture, such as oysters, seaweed and mushrooms. Part of this dislike is cultural and part of it has to do
20 ▸ with the natural signals from the brain that warn us when certain foods may be unsafe to eat.

④ Pet peeves can seriously affect our relationships with family, friends, classmates and co-workers. Understanding the pet peeves of others around us can prevent these relationships from deteriorating, making life less stressful and more pleasant.

Words: pet peeves いらいらさせるもの　annoying 迷惑な　disgusting 実に嫌な　universal 普遍的な
scratching 引っかいている　psychological 心理的な　frequency 周波数　slimy ぬるぬるした

A Vocabulary Builder

次の単語の本文中での意味を、a. 〜 c. の中から1つずつ選びましょう。

1. canals (line 15):   a. passengers   b. passages   c. partners

2. amplify (line 16):   a. shorten   b. harden   c. louden

3 texture (line 18):   a. feel   b. culture   c. poison

4. deteriorating (line 24):   a. improving   b. developing   c. worsening

B Comprehension Questions

完成した英文が本文の内容に合うように、a. 〜 c. の中から最も適切なものを1つずつ選びましょう。

1. Slow drivers fall under the category of (**a.** an annoying pet peeve   **b.** a disgusting pet peeve   **c.** a universal pet peeve).

2. In the study, subjects gave a better rating when they thought the sound came from (**a.** chalk on a blackboard   **b.** a musical piece   **c.** both **a.** and **b.**)

3. According to the passage, many people dislike slimy foods because they (**a.** taste odd   **b.** look unusual   **c.** have a strange texture).

4. (**a.** Sharing our pet peeves with others   **b.** Being aware of others' pet peeves   **c.** Ending some of our relationships) can make life less stressful.

C Paragraph Summaries

次の英文が表している本文の段落番号を（　）に記入しましょう。

(　　) The body's natural warning system as well as culture explain why many people have a distaste for slimy foods.

(　　) Understanding others' annoyances can help us maintain relationships.

(　　) While the majority of pet peeves go unnoticed, there are a few that almost everyone considers annoying or disgusting.

(　　) There are several physical and psychological reasons why people almost universally dislike the sound of fingernails scratching a chalkboard.

Listening

ng の発音に注意して聞こう

英語には -ng の形で終わる単語が数多くあります。g という文字があることから、例えば sing を「シング」のように発音しがちですが、/g/ の音は関係ありません。日本語の「看護（かんご）」や「円（えん）」の「ん」を発音する時のような音になるので注意しましょう（ng は発音記号では /ŋ/ となります）。

Task ── 下線部の発音に注意して英文を聞き、リピートしましょう。──

1. It took me a lo<u>ng</u> time to finish readi<u>ng</u> this novel.

2. We're goi<u>ng</u> swimmi<u>ng</u> in the river tomorrow morni<u>ng</u>.

3. I saw a you<u>ng</u> boy practici<u>ng</u> soccer in the parki<u>ng</u> lot.

A 会話を聞き、下のイラストの内容が出てくる順番に 1 ～ 4 の番号を（　）に記入しましょう。

　（　　）　　　　（　　）　　　　（　　）　　　　（　　）

B もう一度会話を聞き、（　）に単語を記入しましょう。

A: I wish that guy would stop talking so ¹(　　　　　　) on his smartphone. It's very annoying.

B: That's one of my pet peeves, too. ²(　　　　　　), we get off at the next station.

A: Right. … By the way, what are some of your other pet peeves?

B: Well, I hate it when people sneeze* without ³(　　　　　　) their mouth.

A: Yeah, that's pretty ⁴(　　　　　　).

B: And I think it's terrible when people just throw their ⁵(　　　　　　) on the sidewalk.

A: I totally agree. I once saw a couple throwing a ⁶(　　　　　　) ⁷(　　　　　　) into a river.
Can you believe it?

* sneeze くしゃみをする

C 質問を聞き、最も適切な答えを a. ～ c. の中から 1 つずつ選びましょう。

1. a. b. c.　　　2. a. b. c.　　　3. a. b. c.　　　4. a. b. c.

Speaking

《話題を変える》表現を使って会話をしよう

会話では、話題が変わることが日常茶飯事です。以下は、話題を変えたいときに使える表現です。話が一区切りつくところを見計らって、タイミング良く切り出しましょう。

> by the way「ところで」、speaking of ...「…と言えば」、that aside「それはさておき」、to change the subject「話は変わりますが」、it's off the subject, but ...「余談ですが…」

Ex.

A: Did you hear that Tom joined a baseball team recently?

B: I can't believe it! He hates sports. What made him do that?

A: He was really impressed when a Japanese player became a star in the U.S.

B: I see. Oh, **speaking of baseball**, are you still looking for a part-time job? My father runs a batting center, and he's looking for new staff.

A: Yes, that would be great!

A 話題を変えるときの表現を1つ使って次の会話を完成させましょう。完成後、ペアで練習しましょう。

A: What are the first three things you do when you get up in the morning?

B: Let's see. … First, I _____. After that, I _____

_____. And then I usually _____.

A: _____, do you always go to bed at the same time?

B: _____.

B 次の質問についてパートナーと会話をしましょう。

	👤 Me	👤 My Partner
1. What do you usually have for breakfast?		
2. How many hours do you sleep every night?		
3. What are three things you usually do before bed?		
4. What's one of your bad habits?		
5. What's one of your good habits?		

Writing

《頻度》を表す表現を使って英文を書こう

頻度とは、ある事柄がどの程度よく行われるかを表す概念です。p.21 で提示したものに加え、英語では以下のような表現が使われます。

> **always** いつも　**usually** たいてい　**X times a day [week, month, year]** 1 日（1 週間・1 ヵ月・1 年）に X 回
> **on Sundays** 毎週日曜日に　**on Saturday mornings** 毎週土曜日の朝に　**every weekend** 毎週末
> **once in a while** たまに

Ex.

I never used to care about my health, but things changed when I had a medical check-up two months ago. My doctor told me that I needed to exercise more. So, I started going to the gym. I **usually** work out **three times a week**, and I **sometimes** do hot yoga, too. It's amazing how much more energy I have now.

Task　学期中の 1 週間の過ごし方についてのパラグラフを書きましょう。

Step 1　学期中にすることを挙げ、それぞれどの程度の頻度で行うのかをまとめましょう。

Action （行動）	How often? （頻度）	Additional Information （行動）
ex) go to the gym	three times a week	lots of young people work out there

Hint: アルバイトをする、レポートを書く、サークル活動をする

Step 2　Step 1 のアウトラインをもとにパラグラフを書きましょう。

These are some things that I do during a typical week when classes are in session. For one thing, I _____

_____. *Another thing I do is* _____

_____.

And finally, _____

_____.

Unit 4

Social Behavior

人間は社会的な存在であり、他者と協働しながら集団の中で日々の生活を営んでいます。さまざまな社会的な集団の中における人の振る舞いについて研究する心理学の一分野を社会心理学と呼びます。この Unit では、社会心理学に関連するトピックについて英語で理解したり表現したりする練習をしましょう。

Warm-Up Questions

個人作業とグループ作業の良い点と悪い点を以下の表にまとめましょう。

	👍 Good points	👎 Bad points
Individual work		
Group work		

Which do you prefer? (✓)　☐ Individual work　　☐ Group work

パラグラフごとのメインアイデアを捉えよう

英語のパラグラフには原則として1つのメインアイデアがあります。それぞれのパラグラフのメインアイデアを一言で言うと何になるかを意識して読むことが大切です。段落の最初と最後の文に特に注目しましょう。

Social Loafing

1　In 1913, a French engineer named Maximilien Ringelmann conducted an experiment in which individual people were asked to pull on a rope. He then asked
5▸ those same individuals to pull on the rope in groups of two, three and eight. Ringelmann found that when participants pulled with a group, they made less effort than they did when they pulled on their own. This is known as the Ringelmann effect, or social loafing—the tendency for individual productivity to decrease as group size increases.

10▸ 2　Social loafing doesn't just happen in tug of war games. It may happen on teams in the workplace, on sports teams, or in groups working on assignments or projects at school. People who feel that they can clap more softly in a crowd, or that they don't need to vote because they think it won't make a difference, are also considered to be social loafers.

15▸ 3　The bigger the group, the harder it is to evaluate individual performance. And if no one is paying attention to what others are or aren't doing, it's easier for someone to keep loafing, knowing that the work will eventually get done anyway. There are, however, people who *do* notice when someone on their team isn't doing their share of the work. This can be demotivating, and it usually results in tension and struggles within the team.

20▸ 4　How can social loafing be discouraged? First, it's important to remember that people are more motivated to contribute when their efforts are appreciated. Keeping the group size between three and five members whenever possible, setting clear rules and guidelines, and assigning particular tasks to each group member are all effective ways of achieving less social loafing and more productivity.

> **Words:** social loafing 社会的手抜き　participants 参加者　productivity 生産性　tug of war 綱引き　demotivating やる気を失わせるような　struggles 苦労　contribute 貢献する

A Vocabulary Builder

次の単語の本文中での意味を、a. ～ c. の中から１つずつ選びましょう。

1. tendency (line 9):   a. impossibility   b. warning   c. likelihood

2. evaluate (line 15):   a. judge   b. accept   c. classify

3. discouraged (line 20):   a. disheartened   b. prevented   c. discovered

4. appreciated (line 21):   a. improved   b. examined   c. valued

B Comprehension Questions

完成した英文が本文の内容に合うように、a. ～ c. の中から最も適切なものを１つずつ選びましょう。

1. Ringelmann discovered that people generally (**a.** prefer to work in small groups **b.** dislike working in groups **c.** make less effort in a group situation).

2. A student who (**a.** doesn't study for tests **b.** doesn't contribute during group work **c.** often oversleeps and is absent from classes) is a social loafer.

3. An individual's performance is harder to evaluate when (**a.** their team has many members **b.** their team has few members **c.** they're working alone).

4. A suggestion to avoid social loafing is to (**a.** encourage team members to socialize more **b.** give individual work assignments **c.** eliminate teamwork).

C Paragraph Summaries

次の英文が表している本文の段落番号を（　）に記入しましょう。

(　) When the contributions of individual members of a team are recognized, the team's performance as a whole is likely to increase.

(　) It's easier for social loafing to go unnoticed in larger groups. Anyone who sees it, however, may become less motivated to complete the task.

(　) Social loafing may occur in a variety of social settings.

(　) The tendency to make less effort when working in a team compared to working individually is known as social loafing.

Listening

音声変化を意識して聞こう① 同化

Did you stay up late? という文の下線部は、通例「ディッドゥ」「ユー」ではなく「ディヂュー」のように発音されます。この現象を「同化」と呼び、主に2つ目の単語が you や your のときに生じます。

Task ——下線部の発音に注意して英文を聞き、リピートしましょう。——

1. Why don't you join us?
2. How's your business?
3. Did you get up early?
4. I miss you so much.
5. She wants your email address.
6. We need your help.

A 会話を聞き、下のイラストの内容が出てくる順番に1～4の番号を（　）に記入しましょう。

　　（　　）　　　　　　　（　　）　　　　　　　（　　）　　　　　　　（　　）

B もう一度会話を聞き、（　）に単語を記入しましょう。

A: How ¹(　　　　　) ²(　　　　　　　) project go, Mike? You were the team leader, right?

B: Yes. ³(　　　　　　), it started off badly. One day, a member was playing games on his smartphone. On another day, a different member was sleeping at her desk.

A: What did you say to them?

B: Nothing. Instead, I ⁴(　　　　　) a meeting. I gave them all individual tasks and a work ⁵(　　　　) schedule. Then we met twice a week to discuss our progress.

A: And what ⁶(　　　　) after that?

B: Everyone stayed focused and motivated, and the project was a huge ⁷(　　　　　).

C 質問を聞き、最も適切な答えを a. ～ c. の中から1つずつ選びましょう。

1. a. b. c.　　　2. a. b. c.　　　3. a. b. c.　　　4. a. b. c.

Speaking

《提案》の表現を使って会話をしよう

相手に「〜したらどうですか」と提案をする際、英語には以下のような表現があります。

I think you should *do*... 「…した方が良いと思います」、Why don't you ...? [Why not ...?] 「…したらどうですか」、It may be a good idea to ... 「…しても良いかもしれません」、How about *doing*? 「…するのはどうですか」

Ex.

A: Ben, you look a little worried today. Is everything OK?

B: No. I accidentally deleted the PowerPoint file for our group presentation.

A: Oh dear! … I know it's not easy, but **I think you should** tell your group members the truth.

B: Yeah, you're right. I'll tell them right away.

A 《提案》の表現を 2 つ使って次の会話を完成させましょう。完成後、ペアで練習しましょう。

A: I'm so nervous about my presentation tomorrow. Can you give me some advice?

B: OK … _____.

A: That's a good idea. I'll do that. Do you have any other suggestions?

B: Well, _____.

A: Oh, I never thought of that. That's a terrific suggestion. Thank you.

B: No problem. Let me know how it goes.

B 次の質問についてパートナーと会話をしましょう。

*white lie たわいのない（罪のない）嘘

	Me	My Partner
1. How often do you text friends or family members?		
2. What club activities did you do in high school? Are you in any clubs now?		
3. Would you like to be the leader of a club or sports team? Why or Why not?		
4. Do you think it's sometimes OK to tell a white lie*? If so, when?		

Writing

《条件》を表す表現を使って英文を書こう

英文を書く際、《条件》を表す場面が多くあります。《条件》と聞くと if がすぐに思い浮かびますが、英語にはその他にもさまざまな表現があります。どのような条件を表すのかに着目して使いこなしましょう。

if S+V もし S が V ならば　　**unless S+V** もし S が V でなければ　　**once S+V** いったん S が V したら
as long as S+V S が V する限り、S が V さえすれば　　**now that S+V** 今や S が V なので

Ex.

If you want to improve your English speaking ability, the most important thing is to enjoy communication. Don't be afraid of making mistakes, and focus on what you want to express. **Once** you start feeling more confident, you should pay more attention to accuracy. Your speaking ability will definitely improve **as long as** you enjoy using English.

POINT 一口に《条件》と言っても、ニュアンスや使われる状況・場面が異なるので注意しましょう。

Task グループワークのリーダーを任された友人の Kelly から、メンバーのコミュニケーションをどのように図るべきかについて相談を受けました。上の表現を最低 1 つ使いながら、アドバイスの e メールを書きましょう。

Step 1 以下のフレームを使ってどのような対応をすべきかを整理しましょう。

Action
Step 1
Step 2
Step 3

Hint: 自己紹介をする、一緒に食事をする、グループを 2、3 人の小グループに分ける、みんなの意見を尊重する、肯定的になる、リラックスした雰囲気を保とうとする

Step 2 Step 1 のアウトラインをもとに Kelly に e メールを書きましょう。

Hi Kelly,

Here are a few suggestions that you might use to improve communication among your group members. First,_____

_____

_____. Good luck!

University Life

2020 年に初めて、新型コロナウィルス感染症が世界を襲いました。その影響は大学にも及び、従来の対面型授業に加えてオンラインによる遠隔授業が導入されるなど、大学のあり方に大きな変革が生じました。この Unit では、オンライン学習や大学生活について英語で理解したり表現したりする練習をしましょう。

Warm-Up Questions

次の質問に対して英語で答えましょう。

1. What are some good and bad points of online classes? List three for each.

👍 Good points   👎 Bad points

•	•
•	•
•	•

2. Which do you prefer, online classes or face-to-face classes? Why?

_____

《列挙》の表現に着目して英文を読もう

以下の英文では、オンライン学習のメリットとデメリットが述べられています。それぞれに対して複数のポイントが列挙されているので、also や in addition、another といった表現に注目して内容を捉えましょう。

Online Learning

[1] In today's world, online learning has become a necessary resource for students and educational institutions all over the world. Like all types of learning, however, online learning comes with its own set of advantages and disadvantages.

5 ▸ [2] On the positive side, online learning is an efficient way of delivering high-quality lessons to students beyond traditional textbooks, through digital resources such as videos, PDF's and podcasts. In addition, online education saves students time by allowing them to attend classes from the location of their choice. Students can also record lectures and view them at their convenience. Online learning reduces the

10 ▸ students' financial burden, too. Tuition fees are generally lower than they are for physical learning environments. Many students also save money on transportation, meals and housing.

[3] On the negative side, one of the biggest challenges of online education is finding ways to keep students focused on the screen for long periods of time. There is also a

15 ▸ greater chance for students to be distracted by social media or other online sites. The challenge for teachers, therefore, is to keep their lessons engaging, fast-paced and interactive. The technical issue of Internet connectivity can also be problematic. An inconsistent Internet connection may result in a lack of continuity in learning. Another disadvantage is the lack of face-to-face interaction among students and teachers, which

20 ▸ may result in a sense of isolation for some students. This can be very demotivating, and may even lead to students leaving school.

[4] There is little doubt that online learning is here to stay and will continue to develop. The key, therefore, is to continue to find ways to improve it and to minimize its disadvantages as much as possible.

Words: tuition fees 学費　distracted 注意をそらされる　inconsistent 不安定な　continuity 継続性

A Vocabulary Builder

次の単語の本文中での意味を、a. ～ c. の中から１つずつ選びましょう。

1. efficient (line 5):　　　a. effective　　　b. simple　　　c. inexpensive

2. burden (line 10):　　　a. gain　　　b. planning　　　c. load

3. engaging (line 16):　　　a. meeting　　　b. interesting　　　c. connected

4. isolation (line 20):　　　a. loneliness　　　b. admiration　　　c. independence

B Comprehension Questions

完成した英文が本文の内容に合うように、a. ～ c. の中から最も適切なものを１つずつ選びましょう。

1. In general, online classes (a. are less expensive than　b. are more expensive than c. cost about the same as) in-person classes.

2. (a. Taking class attendance　b. Maintaining student concentration　c. Learning students' names) is stated as a problem that online teachers often face.

3. The passage stresses the importance for teachers to make their online lessons (a. shorter than usual　b. as simple as possible　c. interactive).

4. The passage suggests that online learning will (a. likely become less popular b. eventually replace all physical classrooms　c. continue to grow).

C Paragraph Summaries

次の英文が表している本文の段落番号を（ ）に記入しましょう。

( )　Maintaining students' focus, overcoming Internet connection problems, and preventing students from feeling isolated are all challenges of online learning.

( )　Online learning has emerged as an important teaching method worldwide.

( )　The future of online education lies in building on the positives and finding ways to reduce the negatives.

( )　Online education can provide students with first-rate education regardless of time or place, save students time, and lower their financial load.

Listening

音声変化を意識して聞こう② 音の連結

英語では、《子音+母音》の音の並びになったとき、両者がくっ付いて発音されます。例えば、I'm on it.（その話に乗った）は、「アイマニットゥ」のように聞こえます。

Task ——下線部の発音に注意して英文を聞き、リピートしましょう。——

1. Can I use it?

2. Have a nice day!

3. Take it easy.

4. Where am I?

*use, have, take の最後の e は発音されないため、いずれも子音で終わります。

A 会話を聞き、下のイラストの内容が出てくる順番に 1 ～ 4 の番号を（　）に記入しましょう。

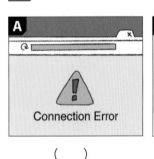

（　　）　　　　　（　　）　　　　　（　　）　　　　　（　　）

B もう一度会話を聞き、（　）に単語を記入しましょう。

A: How are your online studies [1](　　　　　　　) this year, Ken?

B: Very well. I had a few [2](　　　　　　) [3](　　　　　　　) with my Internet connection at first, but it's working fine now.

A: Are you enjoying your English class?

B: Yes. The teacher divided us into small groups, so we can practice speaking together. Compared to on-campus classes, we're less [4](　　　　　) [5](　　　　　　) making mistakes.

A: That's great! [6](　　　　　) I really like is not having to ride crowded trains every day. And that gives me more time and [7](　　　　) to study.

C 質問を聞き、最も適切な答えを a. ～ c. の中から 1 つずつ選びましょう。

1. a. b. c.　　　2. a. b. c.　　　3. a. b. c.　　　4. a. b. c.

36

Speaking

《言い換え》の表現を使って会話をしよう

会話の際、自分の言いたいことが十分に相手に伝わらないことがあります。その場合、別な表現を使って言い換えることが求められます。以下は言い換えのときに使える表現です。

> In other words, ... 「言い換えると」、That is to say, ... 「すなわち」、To put it a different way, ... 「別の言い方をすると」、What I'm trying to say is, ... 「私が言おうとしていることは」

Ex.

A: Did you hear that the university is going to promote BYOD from next year?

B: What's BYOD? I've never heard of it.

A: It stands for Bring Your Own Device. **In other words**, the university will encourage students to bring their own computers or tablets to class, instead of using computer rooms.

B: Most students have their own devices nowadays, so I think it's a good idea.

A: I agree, but they'll make our bags heavier.

A 《言い換え》の表現を 1 つ使って次の会話を完成させましょう。完成後、ペアで練習しましょう。

*obsolete 老朽化した

A: Do you think school buildings will become obsolete* one day?

B: Obsolete? What do you mean by that?

A: _____, do you think all learning will be done online in the future,

so that physical buildings won't be necessary anymore?

B: Oh, I see. Umm, _____, because _____

_____.

B 次の質問についてパートナーと会話をしましょう。

	Me	My Partner
1. What are two big differences between life as a high school student and life as a university student?		
2. Are you enjoying your university life more or less than your high school life? Why?		

Writing

《賛成・反対》の表現を使って英文を書こう

あるテーマに対して賛成・反対の立場を表す際、以下のような表現を使うことができます。

I'm for [against] …. 私は…に賛成［反対］です　**I [totally, completely/partially] agree [disagree] with** …. 私は…に［完全に／部分的に］賛成［反対］です　**I agree in principle.** 大筋では賛成です **I'm generally in favor of** … 私は概して…に賛成です

Ex.

I'm against the idea of students bringing their own devices to class. One of the major reasons is the battery charge problem. For example, if students have three classes in a row in which they need to use their computers, their batteries will likely run out. And there aren't enough outlets available on our campus now, either.

POINT 単に賛成か反対かを述べるだけでなく、totally や partially といった副詞を使うことでニュアンスを調整できます。

Task 「紙の教科書を廃止し、デジタル教科書にすべきだ」という主張に対する意見を書きましょう。

Step 1 紙の教科書とデジタル教科書のメリットとデメリットを整理しましょう。

	Reasons for	Reasons against
Paper textbooks		
Digital textbooks		

Step 2 Step 1 のアウトラインをもとにパラグラフを書きましょう。

I_____ the idea of abolishing paper textbooks and replacing them with digital textbooks. In my opinion,_____

_____

_____

_____

Culture and Traditions

和食や着物、歌舞伎、アニメなど、日本には世界に誇る独自の文化や伝統があります。その中でも近年世界中の人々を魅了しているのがマンガです。今や英語で manga と言っても伝わるようになりました。この Unit では、文化や伝統について英語で理解したり表現したりする練習をしましょう。

Warm-Up Questions

次の質問に対して英語で答えましょう。

1. Do you like reading manga? Why or why not?

   _____

   _____

2. Can you name three popular manga?

   _____

   _____

Reading

《時》を表す表現に着目して流れをつかもう

英語の文章には、時間的順序に沿って物事を説明するタイプのものがあります。このような英文を読む際は、年や時代、歴史上の出来事、... years later や over time、by ...、today といった表現に注目しましょう。

Manga

① When we think about Japanese culture, one of the first things that comes to mind is manga. Many people believe that manga is a fairly recent form of storytelling, but its origin can actually be traced back many centuries.

5 ② It is widely thought that the first manga in Japan were produced by several artists in the 12th and 13th centuries in a series of drawings of rabbits, frogs and other animals called *Choju-Giga* (Scrolls of Frolicking Animals). The technique the artists used for drawing a character's legs to simulate running is still used by many manga artists today. *Toba Ehon*, a book of drawings sold by a publisher in Osaka in the 18th century, was the

10 first manga book available to the general public. The book featured drawings with an accompanying story about the lives of ordinary people in the Edo period (1603-1867). The term "manga" first appeared in a book called *Shiji no Yukikai* (Four Seasons) in 1798.

③ Manga became mainstream in Japan in the years following World War II. Inspired

15 by American comics, Japanese manga artists created their own unique style. By the 1960's, manga had become so popular that manga magazines were being published on a weekly and monthly basis. It was also around this time that Machiko Hasegawa introduced the large eyes that we are so accustomed to seeing in manga and anime today.

20 ④ Over time, manga turned into entire books, including series consisting of as many as 20 volumes. And as children became adults, manga series focusing on everything from business and politics to history and relationships also began to appear. Today, manga remains an important part of Japanese culture, with no reason to believe that its popularity will fade anytime soon.

Words: traced back さかのぼる　featured 大きく取り上げた　accompanying 別に添えた　on a weekly/monthly basis 1週間／1ヵ月ごとに　politics 政治　fade 次第に消える

40

A Vocabulary Builder

次の単語の本文中での意味を、a. ～ c. の中から 1 つずつ選びましょう。

1. simulate (line 8):   a. look like   b. exercise   c. increase

2. mainstream (line 14): a. important   b. unique   c. common

3. inspired (line 14):   a. weakened   b. taught   c. motivated

4. accustomed to (line 18): a. surprised at   b. used to   c. interested in

B Comprehension Questions

完成した英文が本文の内容に合うように、a. ～ c. の中から最も適切なものを 1 つずつ選びましょう。

1. The technique to simulate a character running was first introduced in (a. *Shiji no Yukikai*
   b. *Choju-Giga*   c. *Toba Ehon*).

2. *Toba Ehon* was a story about (a. Samurai   b. an ordinary family   c. common people)
   living during the Edo period.

3. After World War II, Japanese manga artists (a. were inspired by American comics
   b. copied the drawing style of Americans   c. taught Americans their techniques).

4. Paragraph 4 suggests that manga are (a. beginning to lose their appeal   b. not popular
   among adults   c. enjoyed by people of all ages).

C Paragraph Summaries

次の英文が表している本文の段落番号を（　）に記入しましょう。

(　) Later, manga series began to be published, and manga targeting older readers were
     introduced.

(　) Around the mid-1900's, manga had become very popular, and publications of
     weekly and monthly manga magazines were common.

(　) The first manga drawings were of animals over 800 years ago, while the first manga
     book to include a story appeared more than 200 years ago.

(　) Many people have the false idea that manga is a recent form of storytelling.

Listening

音声変化を意識して聞こう③ 脱落する音

単語の語尾に /t/, /p/, /k/, /d/, /b/, /g/ の音が来るときは、発音の構えは行われますが、音は出ません。例えば、dad は「ダッドゥ」ではなく、「ダッ」のように聞こえるので注意しましょう。

Task ——下線部の発音に注意して英文を聞き、リピートしましょう。——

1. I saw a very bi<u>g</u> do<u>g</u> in the par<u>k</u> yesterday.

2. My ca<u>t</u> was sleeping on the be<u>d</u>.

3. Can you gra<u>b</u> the cu<u>p</u> for me?

A 会話を聞き、下のイラストの内容が出てくる順番に 1 ～ 4 の番号を（　）に記入しましょう。

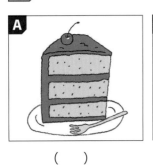

（　　）　　　　　　（　　）　　　　　　（　　）　　　　　　（　　）

B もう一度会話を聞き、（　）に単語を記入しましょう。

A: Aki, have you had any ¹(　　　　　) ²(　　　　　　　　) since you've come to the U.S.?

B: Yes, I'm surprised that people don't ³(　　　　　　) off their shoes in the house.

A: You're right—most people that I know don't. Anything ⁴(　　　　)?

B: Umm…strangers often talk to me at the bus stop, and it's not unusual to see older people wearing ⁵(　　　　) ⁶(　　　　　) and sneakers.

A: Yeah, I ⁷(　　　　) you don't see that much in Japan.

B: Oh, and the food portions* are really big here. I ordered a piece of chocolate cake the other day, and it was HUGE!

* portion（食物の）1 人前

C 質問を聞き、最も適切な答えを a. ～ c. の中から 1 つずつ選びましょう。

1. a. b. c.　　　**2.** a. b. c.　　　**3.** a. b. c.　　　**4.** a. b. c.

Speaking

《許可》を求める表現を使って会話をしよう

「〜してもいいですか」と許可を求める際、英語では以下のような表現を使います。

> Can [May/Could] I ...? / Would [Do] you mind if I ...? / Would it be [Is it] possible for me to ...? / Is it okay if I ...? / I wonder if I could .... / If you don't mind, I'd like to ....

Ex.

A: Maiko, I heard you are going to a kabuki performance this weekend. **I wonder if I could** join you.

B: Sure*. I'm surprised that you're interested in kabuki.

A: I'm not particularly interested, to be honest. But I have to write a report on kabuki for my Japanese culture class.

B: Oh, I see. *答えるときは、Sure. / No problem. / Why not? / Please feel free. といった表現を使います。

A 《許可》を表す表現を 1 つ使って次の会話を完成させましょう。完成後、ペアで練習しましょう。

A: _____ ask you a few questions about New Year's in Japan?

B: _____. What would you like to know?

A: Well, could you explain what *hatsumode* is?

B: Sure. _____.

A: Oh. And do you eat any special foods on New Year's Eve or New Year's Day?

B: _____.

B 次の質問についてパートナーと会話をしましょう。

	Me	My Partner
1. What are two things you did as a family when you were younger?		
2. If you moved to another country, what two things would you miss about Japan?		

Writing

物を描写する英文を書こう

ある物の状態や特徴などを説明することを事物描写と呼びます。このタイプの英文を書く際は、以下の観点を含めると良いでしょう。なお、①〜④の項目はこの順番で書く必要はなく、取捨選択することも可能です。以下の例文を読みながら、英文がどのように構成されているかを確認しましょう。

```
① 種類  ➡  ② 素材  ➡  ③ 用途・働き  ➡  ④ 補足情報・コメント
```

Ex.

A *sensu* is a traditional Japanese folding fan. 《種類》 It looks like a part of a circle, and it is made of paper. 《素材》 Japanese people use it to keep cool during the hot summer months. 《用途 1》 It is also used in art performances such as *rakugo*, and in traditional dances. 《用途 2》 Today, we can buy a wide variety of *sensu* at 100-yen shops. 《補足情報》

POINT 上記の他に、物の由来や分類について説明することもできます。

Task 浴衣（*yukata*）とは何かを説明するパラグラフを書きましょう。

Step 1 以下のフレームを使ってアウトラインを作りましょう。

種類 (type)	
素材 (material)	
用途 (use)	
補足情報・コメント (additional information/comments)	

Step 2 Step 1 のアウトラインをもとにパラグラフを書きましょう。

A *yukata* is _____. It is made of _____

_____. Japanese people _____

_____

_____.

Four Seasons

日本には春・夏・秋・冬の四季があり、それぞれの季節で私たちは自然の風景や食べ物、行事など を楽しみます。一方、世界には日本のような明確な四季が見られない国も多くあります。この Unit では、四季について英語で理解したり表現したりする練習をしましょう。

Warm-Up Questions

次の質問に対して英語で答えましょう。

1. What words come to mind when you think of *sakura*?

　　_____

　　_____

2. Why do you think so many Japanese people love cherry blossoms?

　　_____

　　_____

Reading

未知語の意味を文脈から推測しながら読もう

英文を読んでいて意味がわからない単語に出会った際は、前後の語句や文、その単語の品詞などに注目して意味を推測しましょう。みなさんが既にもっている桜に関する知識も推測をする際に役立ちます。

Sakura—Cherry Blossoms

1　We can find cherry blossoms throughout the world, including countries such as China, Korea and India, as well as in parts of northern Europe. Japan, however, is particularly famous
5▸ for its cherry blossoms, and enjoying and celebrating them in this country is a national pastime. During the cherry blossom season, millions of people head to streets and parks across the country to enjoy their beauty and to
10▸ welcome in the warm spring weather.

2　Different varieties of cherry blossoms bloom at different times. The most common variety of cherry blossom is the *Somei-yoshino*, which is light pink in color. It is often found along rivers, in parks, and on shrine, temple and castle grounds.

3　Every spring, weather forecasters predict the *sakura zensen*, or cherry blossom front,
15▸ as it slowly moves northward. In the southern islands of Okinawa, cherry blossoms open as early as January, while on the northern island of Hokkaido, they bloom as late as May. In major cities in between, including Kyoto, Osaka and Tokyo, the cherry blossom season usually takes place in early April.

4　The cherry blossom season is rather short. After the first blossoms open, full bloom
20▸ is usually reached within about one week. A week later, the blossoms begin to fall from the trees and leaves begin to appear. It is because of this short life cycle that cherry blossoms have come to symbolize the brevity of life in Japan. They are said to be like clouds—appearing all at once, then vanishing just as quickly. Through cherry blossoms, people have learned to appreciate the preciousness and fragility of their own lives.

> **Words:** particularly 特に　pastime 娯楽　varieties 品種　castle grounds 城内　predict 予測する
> appreciate 認識する　preciousness ありがたさ　fragility はかなさ

A Vocabulary Builder

次の単語の本文中での意味を、a. ～ c. の中から 1 つずつ選びましょう。

1. bloom (line 11):   **a.** fall   **b.** change color   **c.** produce flowers

2. symbolize (line 22):   **a.** replace   **b.** represent   **c.** remember

3. brevity (line 22):   **a.** shortness   **b.** beauty   **c.** meaning

4. vanishing (line 23):   **a.** rising   **b.** disappearing   **c.** floating

B Comprehension Questions

完成した英文が本文の内容に合うように、a. ～ c. の中から最も適切なものを 1 つずつ選びましょう。

1. We find cherry blossoms mostly in Asia and (**a.** North America   **b.** South America
    c. northern Europe).

2. The *Somei-yoshino* cherry blossom is (**a.** very rare   **b.** light pink   **c.** only found in
    western Japan).

3. The cherry blossom front (**a.** moves in a northerly direction   **b.** travels quite quickly
    c. predicts the beginning of spring).

4. Cherry blossoms are often compared to clouds because (**a.** they are both light   **b.** they
    are both beautiful   **c.** they both appear and disappear quickly).

C Paragraph Summaries

次の英文が表している本文の段落番号を（ ）に記入しましょう。

(   ) The most common type of cherry blossom in Japan is the *Somei-yoshino.* It is often
        found along streets and in public places such as parks.

(   ) Japanese people love to celebrate the beauty of cherry blossoms, and view them as
        a welcome sign that spring has arrived.

(   ) The short life cycle of cherry blossoms symbolizes the brevity of life in Japan.

(   ) The cherry blossom front starts in Okinawa in January and ends in Hokkaido several
        months later.

Listening

弱く発音される語に注意しよう① and, or, but

会話では、リズムを整えたり、発音をしやすくしたりするために、弱形 (weak form) と呼ばれる形が用いられます。例えば、and は辞書では /ænd/ と記載されていますが、/ən(d)/ と発音されることが多くあります。

Task ——下線部の発音に注意して英文を聞き、リピートしてみましょう。——

1. He loves fish <u>and</u> chips. / She takes cream <u>and</u> sugar in her coffee. /ən(d)/

2. Would you like coffee <u>or</u> tea? / For here <u>or</u> to go? /ər/

3. Meg studied hard for the exam, <u>but</u> she failed. / Sorry, <u>but</u> I have to go. /bə(t)/

 会話を聞き、下のイラストの内容が出てくる順番に 1 〜 4 の番号を記入しましょう。

(   )   (   )   (   )   (   )

B もう一度会話を聞き、（ ）に入る単語を記入しましょう。

A: What's your favorite time of year, Bill?

B: That's easy—late spring ¹(　　　　　　) ²(　　　　　　) fall.

A: And why is that?

B: Well, the ³(　　　　　　) is ideal—not too hot and not too cold.

A: Right. Is that the only reason?

B: Oh, no. I'm retired and I like to ⁴(　　　　　　). Air fares and hotels are much ⁵(　　　　　　) then than they are during the ⁶(　　　　　　) summer months.

A: And places like museums and restaurants are less ⁷(　　　　　　), too, I guess.

 質問を聞き、最も適切な答えを a. 〜 c. の中から 1 つずつ選びましょう。

1. a. b. c.   2. a. b. c.   3. a. b. c.   4. a. b. c.

Speaking

フィラーを効果的に使おう

日本語の会話では、自分の言いたいことがすぐに出てこないときに「えーと」や「うーん」といった表現をはさみます。英語にも、well や umm、I mean、you know、let's see といった表現があり、これらをフィラー（filler）と呼びます。フィラーを使うことで次の表現に移るための時間を稼いだり、内容の言い換えや補足、修正をしたりすることができます。

> **Ex.**
>
> A: What's your favorite school subject?
>
> B: **Let's see**. … I like Japanese history. I'm a great fan of *Shinsengumi*.
>
> A: What's *Shinsengumi*?
>
> B: **Umm** … **How do I say this in English?** … It was a special military force organized by samurai without masters in the late Meiji period, **I mean** Edo period, between 1863 and 1869.
>
> A: Oh, that sounds interesting. Tell me more.

A フィラーを最低 2 つ使って次の会話を完成させましょう。完成後、ペアで練習しましょう。

A: What's a popular seasonal dish in Japan in winter?

B: _____.

A: What is that, exactly?

B: _____.

A: Oh, I see. And how often do you eat it?

B: _____.

B それぞれの季節について好きな点と嫌いな点を書き、パートナーに伝えましょう。完成後、ペアで質問をしましょう。

1. Spring: ☺ In spring, I like _____. ☹ I don't like _____.

2. Summer: ☺ _____. ☹ _____.

3. Autumn: ☺ _____. ☹ _____.

4. Winter: ☺ _____. ☹ _____.

Writing

《列挙》の表現を使って英文を書こう

好きな物や人について文章を書く場合、その理由を複数挙げながら説明することが一般的です。以下は列挙するときによく使われる表現です。

> **first(ly) [first of all / to begin with / in the first place]** 最初に　**second(ly) [in the second place]**
> 2番目に　**third(ly) [in the third place]** 3番目に　**then [next]** 次に　**finally [last(ly)]** 最後に

Ex.

I would like to go to Spain in the future. There are three main reasons. **To begin with**, I have always wanted to see Sagrada Familia in Barcelona. I want to see it being built. **Second,** I want to taste local dishes such as tortillas and pinchos. I'm especially interested in trying paella. **Finally**, I am taking a Spanish class at university now. I would like to use what I've learned to communicate with the people there.

 POINT 理由の後に具体例や自分の経験、追加情報を補うと説得力が増します。

Task ▶ 好きな季節について述べるパラグラフを書きましょう。

Step 1 以下のフレームを使ってアウトラインを作りましょう。

Your favorite season: _____

Reason 1: _____

　　Extra information: _____

Reason 2: _____

　　Extra information: _____

Reason 3: _____

　　Extra information: _____

Step 2 Step 1のアウトラインをもとにパラグラフを書きましょう。

_____ is _____ season. *There are three main reasons.*

_____, _____

_____

_____

_____.

Shopping
Preferences

買い物と言えば、一昔前まではデパートや商店街に行ってするものでした。しかし、インターネットの普及などにより、オンラインショッピングは今や私たちの生活において必要不可欠なものとなりました。この Unit では、買い物について英語で理解したり表現したりする練習をしましょう。

Warm-Up Questions

次の質問に対して英語で答えましょう。

1. Do you shop online? If yes, what kind of things do you buy? If no, why not?

   _____

   _____

2. Which do you think is better, online shopping or in-store shopping? Why?

   _____

   _____

Reading

返り読みをしないよう意識して英文を読もう

ある程度のスピードで英文を読むためには、返り読みを極力しないことが大切です。最初に英文を読む際は、意味の分からない箇所があっても前に戻らず、意味の区切りを意識して最後まで読み通しましょう。

Social Media Influencers

1. Today, nearly half the world's population actively uses social media. Many of these people have turned to social media influencers to help them with their purchasing decisions.

5 ▸ Social media influencers are people who have gained a reputation for their knowledge and expertise on a particular subject. They post regularly on their preferred social media channels, and followers pay close attention to what they say.

2. Needless to say, influencers have become a key component for brands and online sellers. For example, a sporting goods manufacturer might ask a sports influencer to

10 ▸ share a post of himself using their equipment. Or a cosmetics company may have a health and beauty influencer review one of its latest products and post a link to the product on her blog. This marketing approach is often much more effective than traditional paid media such as television commercials and print advertising.

3. Social media influencers have a very trusting and loyal fan base. According to

15 ▸ a reputable global market research company, more than ninety percent of customers trust an influencer more than an advertisement or traditional celebrity endorsement. Customers see a product more favorably when the influencer endorses the product, and are therefore more likely to make a purchase.

4. Brands and Internet shopping businesses love social media influencers for their

20 ▸ ability to generate interest and excitement about their product, boost sales and create opportunities to attract more customers. And when customers feel like they are getting to know influencers on a more personal level, they tend to trust their words and the products they promote. It's no surprise, then, why companies are putting more money into their influencer marketing budgets than ever before.

Words: reputation 評判　expertise 専門的な技術　needless to say 言うまでもなく　print advertising 紙の広告
loyal 忠誠心のある　celebrity endorsement 有名人によるお墨付き

52

A Vocabulary Builder

次の単語の本文中での意味を、a. ～ c. の中から 1 つずつ選びましょう。

1. manufacturer (line 9):　　a. operator　　　b. maker　　　c. manager

2. reputable (line 15):　　a. reasonable　　b. trustworthy　　c. supportive

3. favorably (line 17):　　a. positively　　b. clearly　　c. likely

4. budgets (line 24):　　a. fashions　　b. trends　　c. spending plans

B Comprehension Questions

完成した英文が本文の内容に合うように、a. ～ c. の中から最も適切なものを 1 つずつ選びましょう。

1. Social media influencers are (a. mostly celebrities　b. experts in a specific area
   c. online sellers).

2. The passage states that utilizing social media influencers is often (a. more successful
   b. cheaper　c. less complicated) than using traditional paid media.

3. According to the passage, most consumers (a. regularly switch from one influencer to
   another　b. are often distrustful of influencers　c. are loyal to their influencers).

4. Customers tend to trust an influencer if they (a. share the same interest　b. feel a
   personal connection with them　c. speak with them directly).

C Paragraph Summaries

次の英文が表している本文の段落番号を（ ）に記入しましょう。

(　) Because brands can benefit from utilizing influencers in a number of different ways,
   many of them are increasing their influencer marketing budgets.

(　) Brands and online sellers use social media influencers as a marketing tool.

(　) Before deciding to make a purchase, many consumers look to social media
   influencers.

(　) Most consumers trust social media influencers more than advertisements and
   traditional endorsements by famous people.

弱く発音される語に注意して聞こう② 前置詞

会話では、あえて強調しない限り、前置詞は弱く発音されます（弱形になる）。例えば、to は /túː/ よりも /tə/、of は /ɔ́v/ よりも /ə(v)/ や /ə/、for は /fɔːr/ よりも /fə(r)/ と発音されます。

Task ——下線部の発音に注意して英文を聞き、リピートしてみましょう。——

1. Most <u>of</u> us are not <u>from</u> the Kanto area. /əv/, /frəm/
2. I'd like <u>to</u> talk <u>to</u> you <u>for</u> a few minutes. /tə/, /fər/
3. Can you get a glass <u>of</u> water <u>for</u> me? /ə/, /fə/

・of と for の後ろに続く単語が母音から始まる
　➡ /əv/, /fər/
・of と for の後ろに続く単語が子音から始まる
　➡ /ə/, /fə/

A 会話を聞き、下のイラストの内容が出てくる順番に 1 〜 4 の番号を（　）に記入しましょう。 A 88

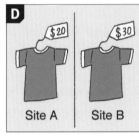

（　　）　　　　　　　（　　）　　　　　　　（　　）　　　　　　　（　　）

B もう一度会話を聞き、（　）に単語を記入しましょう。 A 88

A: Would you like to go to the new outlet ¹(　　　　　　　) this weekend, Tony?

B: Thanks for ²(　　　　　), Linda, but I really don't enjoy going shopping.

A: Oh really? What is it ³(　　　　　) you don't like?

B: Well, for one thing, I ⁴(　　　　　) crowds of people. And I hate waiting in line to make a purchase. That's why I do most of my shopping online.

A: But don't you need to see the ⁵(　　　　　) items that you're thinking of buying?

B: No, not really. I always buy the same ⁶(　　　　　), and I can easily ⁷(　　　　　) prices by checking out several online shopping sites.

C 質問を聞き、最も適切な答えを a. 〜 c. の中から 1 つずつ選びましょう。 A 89-92

1. a. b. c.　　　**2.** a. b. c.　　　**3.** a. b. c.　　　**4.** a. b. c.

Speaking

《正直に自分の気持ちを伝える》表現を使って会話をしよう

会話で自分の気持ちや考えを伝えるとき、以下のような表現を使うことができます。これらの表現は文頭で用いることが多いですが、文の最後に付け加える形で使うこともできます。

> to be honest*、honestly speaking、in all honesty、to be frank*、frankly speaking、actually、to tell the truth
> *to be honest や to be frank の後ろに《with you》を付けることもあります。

Ex.

(A and B are a couple)

A: Wow! That jacket looks great on you!

B: Thanks, but I prefer a tighter fit, **to be honest**.

A: There are some tighter fitting ones over there. Let's check them out.

B: **Actually**, I found a good one online last night, and I ordered it.

A: Seriously? Why didn't you tell me earlier?

 A 上で挙げた表現を 2 つ使って次の会話を完成させましょう。完成後、ペアで練習しましょう。

A: I'm thinking about buying this hat. What do you think? It's $200.

B: _____, I don't really like it.

A: Really? What's wrong with it?

B: Well, _____, _____.

　　 Also, _____.

A: Yeah, you're probably right. Let's keep looking.

B 次の質問について、パートナーと会話をしましょう。

	Me	My Partner
1. Do you prefer to shop alone or with a friend?		
2. What are three things you often buy?		
3. What is the oldest item you have ever bought that you still own? When did you buy it?		
4. If you had a 100,000 yen gift card, what would you buy?		

Writing

《対比・対照》を表す表現を使って英文を書こう

2 つの物を比較・対照しながら説明するタイプの英文を書くときに、以下のような表現を使うことができます。まずは例文を通してそれぞれの使い方を理解した上で、ライティングの際に積極的に使いましょう。

in [by] contrast 対照的に　conversely 逆に　on the contrary それとは反対に	
on the other hand 他方で　while [whereas] S+V ... S が V する一方	

Ex.

Nowadays, more and more people are making cashless payments using smartphone apps. **While** cashless payments are less time-consuming than cash payments, they can lead to overspending because of their ease and convenience. **In contrast**, if you pay by cash, you'll know your spending limitations and will probably be more careful about how you spend your money.

POINT これらの表現を使う際は、2 つの内容が対比や対照の関係になっているかどうかを確認しましょう。

Task 本を地元の書店で買うこととオンラインで買うことを比較するパラグラフを書きましょう。

Step 1 任意の 3 つの観点から両者を比較しましょう。

	Local bookstore	Online bookstore
1	If you find a good book, you can take it home and read it on the same day.	It takes a few days before a book is delivered.
2		
3		

Hint: 価格、時間、持ち運びの負担、購入前の中身の確認、支払い方法、口コミ

Step 2 Step 1 のアウトラインをもとにパラグラフを書きましょう。

Some people like buying books at their local bookstore, while others prefer buying them through online bookstores. If you find a good book at your local bookstore, you can take it home and read it on the same day. On the other hand, it takes a few days _____

_____

_____

_____ .

Safety and Security

人々はこれまで自然災害や犯罪、事故などに対してさまざまな対策や仕組みを構築し、安全で安心な生活を送ることができるよう努力してきました。この Unit では、安全や安心に関するトピックについて英語で理解したり表現したりする練習をしましょう。

Warm-Up Questions

safety や security から連想される語句のマインドマップを作りましょう。

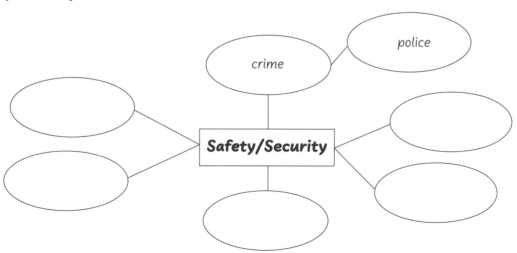

Reading

ビジュアル情報を活用して内容を理解しよう

英文の中には写真やイラスト、図などのビジュアル情報が含まれるものがあります。それらから得られる情報を活用して英文の意味を捉えましょう。以下の英文でも写真が大きなヒントを与えてくれます。

Nightingale Floors

[1] Nobody likes a squeaky floor, so why would anyone want to have one? Back in the Edo period (1603–1868), some Japanese castles and temples were intentionally built with squeaky floors as a way of catching intruders. They were called *uguisu-bari*, or nightingale floors, because the squeaky sound they made with each step sounded oddly similar to the mating call of the normally shy male birds.

[2] During the Edo period, Japan was under the rule of the Tokugawa shogunate. And although there were no wars during this period, there was always the threat from the shogun's feudal lords and other enemies. When Tokugawa Ieyasu built Nijo Castle as his residence in Kyoto, he ordered its builders to install nightingale floors in its hallways. By doing so, guards would immediately be alerted if anyone tried to sneak in.

[3] To install the nightingale floors, the floorboards were loosely fastened to the support beams with metal clamps. The weight of a person walking on the boards caused the clamps to move up and down and rub against two iron nails attaching the clamps to the beams. This friction caused a shrill chirping noise which alerted guards to the presence of spies, thieves and assassins. Guards could even pinpoint an intruder's position based on the size of the noise and the direction it was coming from.

[4] Because it was impossible to walk down the hallways without making the floorboards squeak, guards developed a special walking pattern to alert other guards that it was one of them. As soon as the boards started singing a different tune, they knew it was time to sound the alarm and send in reinforcements.

Words: squeaky キーキー音がする　mating call 求愛鳴き　Tokugawa shogunate 徳川幕府　feudal lords 大名　sneak in もぐりこむ　clamp かすがい（材木と材木とをつなぎとめるために打ち込む、両端の曲がった大きな釘）　shrill chirping noise 鋭い鳴き声のような音　reinforcements 援軍

58

A Vocabulary Builder

次の単語の本文中での意味を、a. 〜 c. の中から1つずつ選びましょう。

1. intruders (line 6): a. unwanted visitors b. guests c. small animals

2. residence (line 12): a. family b. defense c. home

3. friction (line 17): a. rubbing b. weight c. direction

4. thieves (line 18): a. liars b. stealers c. prisoners

B Comprehension Questions

完成した英文が本文の内容に合うように、a. 〜 c. の中から最も適切なものを1つずつ選びましょう。

1. Nightingales use their call (a. to warn others of danger b. when they are hungry c. during mating season).

2. The Edo period was (a. a peaceful chapter in Japanese history b. a period when many wars were fought c. a time of both peace and war).

3. Guards could tell the location of an intruder by the (a. length b. volume c. pitch) of the sound and the direction it was coming from.

4. The phrase "singing a different tune" in the last paragraph means making sounds produced by (a. an unknown person b. a guard c. a special walking pattern).

C Paragraph Summaries

次の英文が表している本文の段落番号を（　）に記入しましょう。

(　) Tokugawa Ieyasu had nightingale floors installed in Nijo Castle.

(　) The squeaky sound of the nightingale floors was caused by metal clamps rubbing against iron nails.

(　) Guards walking the hallways were able to identify themselves to other guards by the pattern of their steps.

(　) In the Edo period, nightingale floors were used in some castles and temples as security systems.

Listening

弱く発音される語に注意して聞こう③ 人称代名詞

人称代名詞の多くが会話において弱形で発音されます。例えば、he ➡ /iː/、him ➡ /əm/、they ➡ /eɪ/、them ➡ /əm/ のように最初の子音が読まれなくなったり、母音が変化したりすることが多くあります。

Task ——下線部の発音に注意して英文を聞き、リピートしてみましょう。——

1. Is he from New Zealand? /iː/

2. Catch you later! /jə/

3. You love her a lot. /ər/

4. What's his phone number? /əz/

5. Please tell them that I'm not coming. /əm/

A 会話を聞き、下のイラストの内容が出てくる順番に 1～4 の番号を（ ）に記入しましょう。

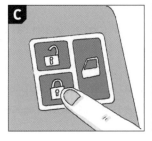

( )   ( )   ( )   ( )

B もう一度会話を聞き、（ ）に単語を記入しましょう。

A: Today I experienced road rage* for the first time. A guy passed me, stopped ¹( ), got out of his car and began shaking his fist at me.

B: That must have been pretty ²( ). What did you do?

A: Well, first I ³( ) my doors. Then when he came next to me, I pointed to my car camera. But that only made ⁴( ) ⁵( ).

B: Oh, my gosh! What happened after that?

A: Luckily, a big mean-looking truck driver got out of his truck and started ⁶( ) at the guy. The guy got scared, ran to ⁷( ) car and drove away. *road rage あおり運転

C 質問を聞き、最も適切な答えを a. ～ c. の中から 1 つずつ選びましょう。

1. a. b. c.   2. a. b. c.   3. a. b. c.   4. a. b. c.

60

Speaking

《過去の出来事を振り返る》表現を使って会話をしよう

「（あの時）…すべきだった」、「…だったに違いない」、「…だったかもしれない」のように、会話では過去の出来事を振り返ることが多くあります。その際、以下のように《助動詞+ have +過去分詞》を使います。

> should have +過去分詞「…すべきだった（のにしなかった）」、may/might have +過去分詞「…だったかもしれない」、must have +過去分詞「…だったに違いない」、could have +過去分詞「…していたかもしれない」

Ex.

A: I heard someone hacked Bob's PC and stole his personal information.

B: Oh, dear. Did he have anti-virus software installed on his computer?

A: He didn't tell me, but he **might** not **have had** any.

B: Well, he **should have been** more careful about his computer security.

A 上で挙げた表現を 2 つ使って次の会話を完成させましょう。完成後、ペアで練習しましょう。

A: I saw a lady fall off the train platform and onto the tracks this morning.

B: Oh, no! _____?

A: She dropped her shoulder bag on the tracks and tried to pick it up with her umbrella.

　　But she slipped and fell. Luckily, two guys helped her back up.

B: That's very dangerous. She might have _____.

　　I think she should have _____.

B 次の質問について、パートナーと会話をしましょう。

	Me	My Partner
1. Do you feel safe walking home at night?		
2. Do you make sure your door is locked before going to bed?		
3. What safety features do you have in your house/apartment?		
4. What do you do to protect your personal data?		

*ex. home security system, outdoor sensor lights, smoke alarm

Writing

《目的》を表す表現を使って英文を書こう

英文を書く際、なぜある行為をしたのかという《目的》を説明することが必要となる場合が多くあります。以下は目的を表すときに使える表現です。

> **(in order) to** *do* / **so as to** *do* / **for the purpose of** *doing* / **with a view to** *doing* …するために
> **so that S+V** S が V するために

Ex.

There are a number of things you can do **in order to protect** yourself from cybercrime. The most basic and easiest way is to install anti-virus software on your computer or smartphone. Remember to update it on a regular basis **so that** it can deal with the latest types of computer viruses. Although it isn't free, it will surely pay off*.　　　*pay off　お金を払うだけの価値がある

 POINT (in order/so as) to do を否定形にする際は、to の前に not を置きます。

Task ▶ 大学における安全対策についてのパラグラフを書きましょう。

Step 1 大学が学生や教職員に対してどのような安全対策を行っているのかを3つ挙げ、その目的または効果についてまとめましょう。

Security Measures（安全対策）	Purpose（目的）/Effect（効果）
Ex. −provides campus security officers	−to keep out intruders

Step 2 Step 1 のアウトラインをもとにパラグラフを書きましょう。

In order to keep students safe and secure, my university uses a number of security measures.

Let me give you three examples. First, _____

_____. Second, _____

_____. Finally, _____

_____

Hints: 防犯カメラ、学生証・職員証、防災訓練、消火器、火災警報機

Unit 10

Smart Technology

インターネットやスマートフォン、タブレット、SNS、動画サイト、ネットショッピング、オンライン授業など、今や私たちの生活は ICT（情報コミュニケーション技術）なしでは成り立たないと言っても過言ではありません。この Unit では、ICT について英語で理解したり表現したりする練習をしましょう。

Warm-Up Questions

次の質問に対して英語で答えましょう。

> Check (✓) the terms you have heard of. What do you think they stand for?

☐ SNS: *social networking service*　　　☐ WWW: _____

☐ ICT: _____　　　☐ USB: _____

☐ PDF : _____　　　☐ LAN: _____

☐ IoT: _____　　　☐ AI: _____

☐ Wi-Fi: _____　　　☐ CAD: _____

用語の定義を正確に捉えて読もう

筆者は、読者にとって馴染みのない用語や新しい概念を使う際に定義を行います。英語では、《説明》+ This is called … や、X refers to Y のような表現がよく用いられます。これらの表現に着目して読んでみましょう。

The Internet of Things

[1]　Today, billions of devices around the world are connected to the Internet, collecting and sharing information. This network is called the Internet of things, or IoT for short. The term is mainly used for
5▸ devices that wouldn't normally be expected to have an Internet connection, and that can communicate with the network without human interaction. Almost any physical object can be transformed into an IoT device. Rice cookers that can be controlled using a smartphone app, smart home security systems and self-driving cars all use IoT technology.

10▸ [2]　In 1982, a Coca-Cola vending machine at Carnegie Mellon University in Pittsburgh became the first Internet-connected appliance. It was able to report when it needed to be restocked and whether or not newly loaded drinks were cold. While the IoT has since played a major part in business and manufacturing, some of the emphasis has shifted more towards making our personal lives safer, more convenient and more comfortable.

15▸ [3]　For the most part, we still control our IoT devices, but ambient intelligence has already begun to change that. Ambient intelligence refers to electronic environments that are sensitive and responsive to the presence of people. The idea that you can interact with Alexa or Siri to set your alarm, stream podcasts or create and play a song list is based on ambient intelligence. In the future, however, ambient intelligence will be
20▸ able to perform such tasks as automatically turning off your smart lights for you when you go to bed, and adjusting the room temperature based on your body heat.

[4]　As with all major technologies, IoT technologies come with their own set of risks. And given the fact that ambient applications will eventually operate largely without our awareness, data sharing and privacy issues will become even more difficult to manage.

Words: vending machine 自動販売機　appliance 電気製品　restocked 補充される　ambient 周囲の、環境の　responsive 反応的な

A Vocabulary Builder

次の単語の本文中での意味を、a. ～ c. の中から1つずつ選びましょう。

1. transformed (line 8):   a. installed   b. changed   c. accepted

2. emphasis (line 13):   a. crisis   b. focus   c. reality

3. environments (line 16): a. images   b. components   c. conditions

4. awareness (line 24):   a. knowledge   b. provider   c. assistance

B Comprehension Questions

完成した英文が本文の内容に合うように、a. ～ c. の中から最も適切なものを1つずつ選びましょう。

1. The IoT is mainly used to describe things that (**a.** need human interaction   **b.** are usually Internet-connected   **c.** aren't usually Internet-enabled).

2. The Carnegie Mellon vending machine (**a.** automatically restocked itself   **b.** was the first Internet-connected device   **c.** reported daily sales).

3. Ambient intelligence aims to enhance the way (**a.** humans   **b.** IoT devices **c.** environments and people) interact with each other.

4. Eventually, ambient intelligence will (**a.** require more interaction with humans   **b.** work mainly without our awareness   **c.** become impossible to manage).

C Paragraph Summaries

次の英文が表している本文の段落番号を（ ）に記入しましょう。

(   ) In the future, ambient intelligence will make decisions and take actions for us based on our preferences.

(   ) The Internet of Things is a network of Internet-connected objects that are able to collect and transfer data without human involvement.

(   ) Risks associated with the IoT include data sharing and privacy issues.

(   ) The IoT has the potential to impact our daily lives in many positive ways.

Listening

弱く発音される語に注意して聞こう④ a/an, the

a や an、the といった冠詞は、会話では弱形で発音されます。a は /ə/、an は /ən/、the は /ðə/ となります。the は次に来る単語が母音で始まっている場合は、/ði/ となるので注意しましょう。

Task — 下線部の発音に注意して英文を聞き、リピートしてみましょう。

1. That's a good idea. / I'll keep it a secret. /ə/

2. I bought an English book. / I'll be back in an hour. /ən/

3. What's the matter? / Put the eggs in the fridge. /ðə/, /ði/

A 会話を聞き、下のイラストの内容が出てくる順番に 1 ～ 4 の番号を ( ) に記入しましょう。

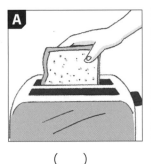

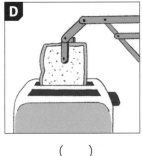

( )   ( )   ( )   ( )

B もう一度会話を聞き、( ) に単語を記入しましょう。

A: Why are you looking at ¹( ) toaster, Bill? Are you going to buy a new one?

B: No, I'm reading about the world's first smart toaster. A software engineer and his friend ²( ) it. They presented it at a computer show in 1990.

A: How ³( ) did it work?

B: It was very simple. They used a computer to turn ⁴( ) ⁵( ) on and off.

A: But it looks like the bread had to be put into the toaster ⁶( ).

B: Right, so in 1991 a robotic ⁷( ) was added which could also be controlled through the Internet. It picked up the bread and dropped it into the toaster.

C 質問を聞き、最も適切な答えを a. ～ c. の中から 1 つずつ選びましょう。

1. a. b. c.   2. a. b. c.   3. a. b. c.   4. a. b. c.

66

Speaking

《明瞭化を求める》表現を使って会話をしよう

会話の中で相手の言ったことを十分に理解できないときは、明瞭化を求めましょう。英語には以下のような表現があります。

> What do you mean by that?「それはどういう意味ですか」、Can you be more specific?「具体的に言ってもらえますか」、Can you give me an example [a few / some examples]?「例を出してもらえますか」、Can you clarify that?「それを詳しく説明してもらえますか」

Ex.

A: It seems that our life has greatly changed after the COVID-19 pandemic.

B: It sure has. We need to be ready to face the VUCA world, don't we?

A: VUCA? **What do you mean by that?**

B: It stands for Volatility*, Uncertainty*, Complexity* and Ambiguity*. It basically means that the world is becoming more and more unpredictable.

* volatility 変動性　uncertainty 不確実性　complexity 複雑性　ambiguity 曖昧性

A 明瞭化を求める表現を1つ使って次の会話を完成させましょう。完成後、ペアで練習しましょう。

A: Do you think technology is a good thing or a bad thing?

B: _____.

A: _____?

B: _____ and _____.

But on the other hand, _____.

B 次の質問について、パートナーと会話をしましょう。

	Me	My Partner
1. What kind of smartphone do you have?		
2. How long have you had your phone?		
3. What do you mainly use it for?		
4. What apps have you installed?		
5. Which app do you use the most often?		

Writing

《例示》を表す表現を使って英文を書こう

英文を書く際、具体例を挙げること (例示) によって自分の意見や主張をより明確に読み手に伝えることができます。以下は主な例示の表現です。

> **for example [instance]** 例えば　　**to illustrate / to give an example** 例を挙げると　　**Let me give you an example.** 例を挙げます　　**Here are some examples.** いくつか例があります　　**like A** A のように

Ex.

A digital tattoo is a record of one's communication on the Internet. It could negatively affect their real life. **To give an example**, suppose you posted some pictures of yourself that others may find to be inappropriate. Even if you delete them, someone might have already copied and posted them on other Internet sites. And if recruiters see them, you may not be invited for a job interview. In order to avoid situations **like this**, we need to be aware that we can't simply press delete on our digital tattoo.

POINT 読み手がクリアに想像したり、自分のこととして受け止めることができたりする例を挙げると効果的です。

Task 'How the IoT will change our lives' というテーマで英文を書きましょう。

Step 1 IoT が私たちの生活にどのような影響を与えるかを整理しましょう。

Our lives now	Our lives with the IoT in the future
We need to adjust the room temperature when using our air conditioner.	Our air conditioner will adjust the room temperature automatically by measuring our body temperature.

Step 2 Step 1 のアウトラインをもとにパラグラフを書きましょう。

The IoT will make our lives easier in the future. For instance, our air conditioner will

_____.

As another example, _____

And finally, _____

Unit 11

Celebrations and Festivals

世界の国々では、さまざまな祝祭が行われています。日本にもひな祭りやこどもの日、七夕、初詣、成人式といった祝祭があります。これらは、人生の節目を祝うことを通して人と人との結びつきを強めてくれます。この Unit では、祝祭について英語で理解したり表現したりする練習をしましょう。

Warm-Up Questions

アメリカに関するクイズに挑戦しましょう。

1. From which country did America become independent?

   a. France　　　　　　**b.** Great Britain　　　　　**c.** Germany

2. When did America become independent?

   a. 1776　　　　　　　**b.** 1867　　　　　　　　**c.** 1911

3. How many states were there when America become independent?

   a. 7　　　　　　　　　**b.** 13　　　　　　　　　**c.** 21

4. Who became the first president of the United States?

   a. George Washington　**b.** Abraham Lincoln　　**c.** Thomas Jefferson

英文を読む前に背景知識を活性化させよう

英文を読む際、みなさんが既にもっている背景知識が理解を助けてくれます。タイトルを見て、自分がそれについてどんなことを知っているのかを思い出してみましょう。キーワードを書き出しても良いでしょう。

American Independence Day

① Independence Day, also called the Fourth of July, celebrates one of the most important events in the history of the United States. On July 4, 1776, the Continental Congress approved the

5 ▶ Declaration of Independence in Philadelphia, announcing the separation of the 13 North American British colonies from Great Britain. Independence from Britain was officially declared, and a new nation was born.

② One of the founding fathers, John Adams, first suggested that Americans should have a "great anniversary festival" to celebrate the nation's independence from Britain.

10 ▶ In a July 3, 1776 letter to his wife Abigail, America's second president wrote, "It ought to be solemnized with pomp and parade, with shows, games, sports, guns, bells, bonfires, and illuminations, from one end of this continent to the other, from this time forward forevermore."

③ The first major celebration of Independence Day took place a year later in

15 ▶ Philadelphia. Ships in the harbor were decorated in the nation's colors of red, white and blue, and their cannons fired a 13-gun salute in honor of the 13 states. The *Pennsylvania Evening Post* newspaper reported that "at night there was a grand exhibition of fireworks (which began and concluded with thirteen rockets) on the Commons, and the city was beautifully illuminated."

20 ▶ ④ Today, many American communities and families have all-day barbecues and picnics on July 4. Others gather in parks for free concerts or line streets to watch parades. At night, people get together to view public fireworks displays. If Adams were still alive to see how July 4 is celebrated today, he would not be disappointed.

Words: Independence Day 独立記念日   Continental Congress 大陸会議   Declaration of Independence 独立宣言
colonies 植民地   founding fathers 建国の父   solemnized （式を挙げて）祝われる   pomp 華やかさ
gun salute 礼砲   in honor of …を讃えて   the Commons コモンズ（社会の中で人々が集う公共の場）

A Vocabulary Builder

次の単語の本文中での意味を、a. ～ c. の中から 1 つずつ選びましょう。

1. approved (line 4):   a. accepted   b. wrote   c. refused

2. declared (line 7):   a. demonstrated   b. commented   c. announced

3. harbor (line 15):   a. moonlight   b. port   c. horizon

4. exhibition (line 17): a. presentation   b. selection   c. collection

B Comprehension Questions

完成した英文が本文の内容に合うように、a. ～ c. の中から最も適切なものを 1 つずつ選びましょう。

1. Another name for Independence Day is (a. the Declaration of Independence   b. the Fourth of July   c. America Day).

2. John Adams was (a. the father of Abigail Adams   b. a famous American writer   c. the second president of the United States).

3. On the first anniversary of America's independence, Philadelphia was beautifully illuminated with (a. bonfires   b. fireworks   b. a full moon and bright stars).

4. If John Adams were still alive, he would be (a. pleased   b. angry   c. disappointed) with the way Independence Day is celebrated today.

C Paragraph Summaries

次の英文が表している本文の段落番号を（　）に記入しましょう。

(　) One of the founding fathers, John Adams, hoped that July 4th would be celebrated from coast to coast every year.

(　) Today, Americans celebrate Independence Day in many of the same ways they did more than two centuries ago.

(　) The United States became independent from Great Britain on July 4, 1776.

(　) To mark the one-year anniversary of the independence of the United States, a great celebration was held in the city of Philadelphia.

Listening

単語アクセントを意識して聞こう

英語は強弱アクセントの言語であり、単語の中に必ずアクセントが置かれる音節があります。正しいアクセントの位置を知らないと聞き取ることができないので、単語を学習する際は必ず発音とセットで覚えましょう。

Task 音声を聞き、アクセントが置かれている部分に下線を引きましょう。音声に続いてリピートしてみましょう。

1. em・ploy・ee
2. vol・un・teer
3. el・e・va・tor
4. tech・nique
5. e・co・nom・ics
6. ki・lo・me・ter

A 会話を聞き、下のイラストの内容が出てくる順番に 1 ～ 4 の番号を（ ）に記入しましょう。

  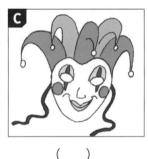 

( )　　　　　( )　　　　　( )　　　　　( )

B もう一度会話を聞き、（ ）に単語を記入しましょう。

A: Hi, Julie. Long time ¹( ) ²( ). How was your holiday?

B: Great! A friend and I went to New Orleans for the Mardi Gras ³( ).

A: Wow! That must have been exciting.

B: It was. We watched a fantastic ⁴( ), with some ⁵( ) floats. And there were free ⁶( ) jazz concerts everywhere.

A: Did you try any interesting food?

B: Yes, we had jambalaya. It's a rice dish with meat or seafood. It was really hot!

Here, I got you a little ⁷( ). It's a Mardi Gras mask.

C 質問を聞き、最も適切な答えを a. ～ c. の中から 1 つずつ選びましょう。

1. a. b. c.　　　2. a. b. c.　　　3. a. b. c.　　　4. a. b. c.

72

Speaking

《予定》を表す表現を使って会話をしよう

一口に《予定》といっても、英語には will や be going to …、現在進行形、be planning to …、be supposed to …、be scheduled to … といったさまざまな表現があります。ニュアンスの違いを押さえて使いましょう。

> **Ex.**
>
> B 38
>
> A: Do you have any plans for the summer vacation?
>
> B: Yeah, I'm **planning** to return to my hometown in Iwate.
>
> A: That's great. Your family must be looking forward to seeing you. How long **are you going to** stay there?
>
> B: A couple of weeks. I'm **scheduled** to attend a job fair at the end of August.
>
> A: Oh, that's right! I completely forgot about job hunting*!
>
> * job hunting 就職活動

A 《予定》を表す表現を使って次の会話を完成させましょう。完成後、ペアで練習しましょう。

A: We're going to graduate soon. How are you _____ celebrate?

B: Well, _____ attend the graduation party, of course. And after that,

I _____ go to Okinawa with a few members of my tennis club.

How about you? What are you planning to do?

A: I _____ and

_____.

B 次の質問について、パートナーと会話をしましょう。

	Me	My Partner
1. When is your birthday?		
2. How do you celebrate birthdays in your family?		
3. Do you give family members or friends birthday presents? For example?		
4. How would you like to celebrate your next birthday?		

Writing

文化固有のものや概念について説明する英文を書こう

文化固有のものや概念について英文を書く際、読み手が理解しやすい説明をすることが求められます。以下の表現を使って説明を行うことで、読み手の理解を助けることができます。

同格の **or** Ex: *Tanabata,* **or** Star Festival / *natto,* **or** fermented beans　**It literally means** … それは文字通り…を意味します　**It roughly means** … それは概ね…を意味します　**It's similar to [like]** … …に似たようなものです

Ex.

In Japan, people celebrate *Kodomo no hi*, **or** Children's Day, on May 5. People hang *koinobori*, which **literally means** "carp streamer," and wish for their children to grow up healthy and strong. This festival was originally for boys, but nowadays it is a celebration for both boys and girls.

POINT 読み手がどのような背景知識をもっているかによって説明の度合いを調整しましょう。

Task 日本の祝祭を1つ選び、それについて述べるパラグラフを書きましょう。

Step 1 以下のフレームを使ってアウトラインを作りましょう。

Festival name	
When and where is it celebrated?	
What do people celebrate?	
How do people celebrate?	

Step 2 Step 1のアウトラインをもとにパラグラフを書きましょう。

In Japan, people celebrate _____, *or* _____ *in English.*

The festival is held _____

_____

_____.

Unit 12

Taking Care of Our Environment

環境問題は人類にとって喫緊の課題です。2015年9月の国連サミットで採択されたSDGs（Sustainable Development Goals: 持続可能な開発目標）には、17の分野にわたる目標が示されおり、持続可能な社会をどのように実現するかを真剣に考え、行動することが私たち一人ひとりに求められています。この Unit では、環境問題について英語で理解したり表現したりする練習をしましょう。

Warm-Up Questions

環境問題に関する以下の語句の意味をペアになって確認しましょう。

1. global warming

   _____

2. air pollution

   _____

3. acid rain

   _____

4. ozone layer

   _____

5. globalization

   _____

6. microplastics

   _____

7. nuclear waste

   _____

8. eco bag

   _____

9. carbon dioxide

   _____

数値に着目して正確に内容を読み取ろう

自然科学系を中心として、多くの文章では数値が用いられます。それぞれの値が何を表すのかを正確に掴むことが重要です。次の英文では、比較表現や nearly、around、under といった副詞や前置詞に着目して読みましょう。

Our Carbon Footprint

1 The term "carbon footprint" is often used to describe the amount of carbon generated by human activities. Our carbon footprint is 16 times greater today

5 ▸ than it was 60 years ago. This has led to one of the most serious problems the world has ever faced—global warming. Reducing our carbon footprint is the most important step that we can take to ensure the well-being of our planet and the life it supports.

2 The 2015 Paris Agreement was a major, historic step in our quest for a fossil-free

10 ▸ future. Nearly 200 countries around the world—including oil-exporting nations— agreed to keep the rise in global temperature below 2°C. This strong move means that we could see an end to fossil fuel use before 2050. The agreement involves much more than simply switching to clean energy. Effectively managing land use is also an important part of the solution.

15 ▸ 3 Globally, the average carbon footprint is around 4.5 tons per person per year, with several countries producing an average of more than 15 tons. Japan's carbon footprint is around 9 tons. In order to prevent a 2-degree rise in global temperature, it is estimated that the average global carbon footprint per year needs to drop to under 2 tons by 2050.

4 What can we do as individuals to reduce our carbon footprint? It may sound cliché,

20 ▸ but small changes can make a big difference. Reducing food waste, taking shorter showers, turning off lights and air conditioners when not in use, eating less meat, buying only necessary items and refusing plastic bags are all ways that will help protect our planet.

Words: carbon footprint カーボンフットプリント（個人や企業の活動を通して排出される二酸化炭素の量）
global warming 地球温暖化 Paris Agreement パリ協定 fossil-free 化石燃料を使わない
oil-exporting nations 石油輸出国 fossil fuel 化石燃料 cliché 陳腐な

A Vocabulary Builder

次の単語の本文中での意味を、a. ～ c. の中から 1 つずつ選びましょう。

1. quest (line 9):   a. request   b. contract   c. search

2. estimated (line 17):   a. known   b. guessed   c. stated

3. waste (line 20):   a. consumption   b. garbage   c. spending

4. refusing (line 22):   a. rejecting   b. purchasing   c. accepting

B Comprehension Questions

完成した英文が本文の内容に合うように、a. ～ c. の中から最も適切なものを 1 つずつ選びましょう。

1. We produce (a. six   b. sixteen   c. sixty) times more carbon than we did sixty years ago.

2. The goal of the Paris Agreement is to (a. limit global warming to below 2°C   b. lower the average global temperature by 2°C   c. increase fossil fuel use).

3. Japan's carbon footprint is about (a. half   b. twice   c. four and a half times) the global average.

4. One way to protect our planet that it mentioned is (a. using less water   b. choosing low energy lighting   c. buying more organic food).

C Paragraph Summaries

次の英文が表している本文の段落番号を（　）に記入しましょう。

(   ) The Paris Agreement was a major step forward in our fight against global warming.

(   ) Small steps by individuals can greatly reduce the global carbon footprint.

(   ) In order to protect our planet and life on it, we must reduce our carbon footprint.

(   ) To keep global temperatures from rising 2°C, the global average carbon footprint needs to be reduced to less than half the current level.

Listening

文アクセントを意識して聞こう

単語の中に強く読まれる音節があるように、文の中にも強く読まれる語があります。一般的には名詞や動詞、形容詞、副詞、疑問詞といった内容語（具体的な内容を表す語）が強く読まれます。

Task ─ 下線部の発音に注意して英文を聞き、リピートしてみましょう。─

1. He <u>told</u> me the <u>way</u> to the <u>stadium</u>.
2. I <u>tried</u> to <u>call</u> you <u>many</u> <u>times</u>.
3. I <u>met</u> a <u>woman</u> who was <u>kind</u> and <u>intelligent</u>.

A 会話を聞き、下のイラストの内容が出てくる順番に 1 〜 4 の番号を（　）に記入しましょう。

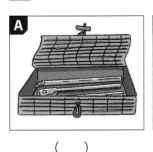
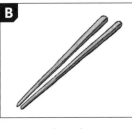
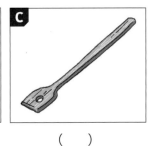
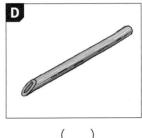

（　　）　　　　（　　）　　　　（　　）　　　　（　　）

B もう一度会話を聞き、（　）に単語を記入しましょう。

A: That's a nice pencil case you have there, Anne.

B: It's not a pencil case. I ¹(　　　　　　　) it my eco-friendly case. I'm trying to make my carbon footprint ²(　　　　　).

A: Cool! Can you show me what's ³(　　　　　)?

B: Sure. … This is my reusable ⁴(　　　　　). … And this is my reusable coffee stirrer. … And you know how much I love Japanese food, so I also have …

A: … reusable ⁵(　　　　　).

B: That's right. Everything is ⁶(　　　　　) ⁷(　　　　　) bamboo.

C 質問を聞き、最も適切な答えを a. 〜 c. の中から 1 つずつ選びましょう。

1. a. b. c.　　　2. a. b. c.　　　3. a. b. c.　　　4. a. b. c.

Speaking

《依頼を断る》表現を使って会話をしよう

日本語、英語を問わず、誰かから依頼されたことを断るのはひと苦労です。以下のような表現をレパートリーに入れておくことで、場面や状況に応じた断り方が可能となります。

Thank you, but I can't. / I'm sorry, but ... / I wish I could, but ... / I'd really love to, but ... / Thanks for asking, but ... / It's nice of you to ask, but ... / Thank you very much for the offer, but ...

Ex.

B 49

A: Hey, Tina. Our group is giving a presentation at city hall this Saturday on what we can do to achieve SDGs in our local community. I wonder if you could come and listen to it.

B: **I'd really love to, but** I promised my sister that I'd babysit for her on Saturday.

A: Okay, no problem. I'll see you later.

A 依頼を断る表現を1つ使って次の会話を完成させましょう。完成後、ペアで練習しましょう。

A: Hi, _____. Some of us in the class are going to do a beach cleanup this weekend.

　Would you like to join us? We're having a barbecue party after.

B: _____?

A: Sunday afternoon. We're all going to meet at _____ at:_____.

B: _____, but _____.

A: _____. Maybe next time.

B 以下のそれぞれの項目をどの程度普段の生活で実践しているかを、always、usually、often、sometimes、occasionally、seldom、never の中から選び、パートナーと会話をしましょう。

☺☺☺How Green Are You?☺☺☺	Me	My Partner
1. Do you use your own shopping bag?		
2. Do you pick up and throw away other people's trash?		
3. Do you use reusable chopsticks?		
4. Do you turn off the water when brushing your teeth?		

Writing

《結果》を表す表現を使って英文を書こう

「温室効果ガスの増加の結果、地球温暖化が引き起こされる」のように、ある事象が原因となってある結果が生まれるという関係を説明することは多くあります。以下は《結果》を表すときに使える表現です。

結果として	**As a result (of ~) ... As a consequence, ... Consequently, ...**
~になる・至る	... **lead(s) to ~ ... result(s) in ~**

Ex.

B 50

Every day, humans emit what are called greenhouse gases such as carbon dioxide (CO_2) and methane*. This will **lead to** global warming, or the gradual* rise in the average temperature.
As a result, we now face various serious problems such as the melting of the polar ice caps* and a rise in sea levels.

* methane メタン   gradual 徐々の   the melting of the polar ice caps 極地の氷が解けること

Task マイクロプラスチック（microplastics）問題について説明するパラグラフを書きましょう。

Step 1 図の①〜④を説明する英文を書きましょう。必要に応じてリサーチをしましょう。

① People throw plastic bottles, _____, _____, _____, etc. into the ocean.

② Plastic breaks down into tiny pieces and fish think they're _____.

③ _____ _____ from the poison.

④ _____ and _____.

* microplastics: small pieces of plastic less than 5 mm long

Step 2 Step 1 のアウトラインをもとにパラグラフを書きましょう。その際、上に挙げた《結果》を表す表現を最低 1 つは使いましょう。

Plastic actually contains many poisonous chemicals. Unfortunately, many people throw plastic bottles,_____, etc. into the ocean. Over time, the plastic
_____. *These tiny pieces are called_____.*
Fish think they're _____. They_____.
Finally,_____.

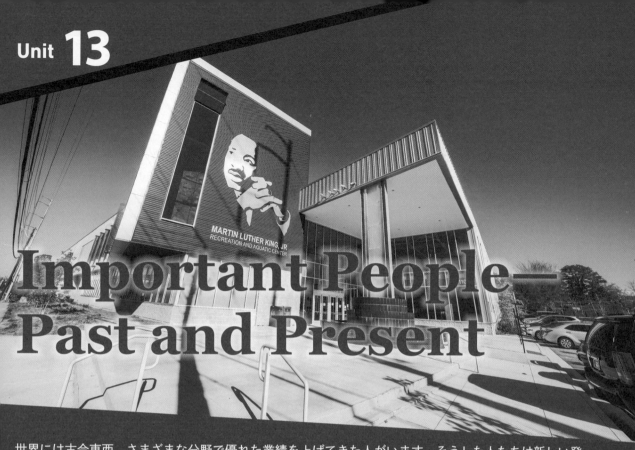

Unit 13

Important People— Past and Present

世界には古今東西、さまざまな分野で優れた業績を上げてきた人がいます。そうした人たちは新しい発見や発明をしたり、私たちの社会のあり方を変えたりしたりしました。偉人以外にも、私たちの身の回りにはさまざまな人々がいます。この Unit では、人物について英語で理解したり表現したりする練習をしましょう。

Warm-Up Questions

次の人物に関連する語句を a ～ g の中から 1 つずつ選び、線で結びましょう。

1. Leonardo da Vinci　　　　　•　　　•　　a. iPS cells

2. Audrey Hepburn　　　　　　•　　　•　　b. *Roman Holiday*

3. Shinya Yamanaka　　　　　　•　　　•　　c. *Mona Lisa*

4. Florence Nightingale　　　　•　　　•　　d. first controlled flight

5. Martin Luther King Jr.　　　•　　　•　　e. *The Marriage of Figaro*

6. Wright Brothers　　　　　　•　　　•　　f. modern nursing

7. Wolfgang Amadeus Mozart　•　　　•　　g. "I Have a Dream" speech

Reading

指示語に着目して内容を読み取ろう

英文を読む際は、this や that、it などの指示語が指す内容を正確に掴むことが重要です。this や that は、指示代名詞として単独で用いられたり、《this / that ＋名詞》の形で指示形容詞として用いられたりします。

Charles Darwin

1　Charles Darwin was born in England and lived from 1809 to 1882. In 1831, he set off on a five-year scientific voyage on *HMS* Beagle as the ship's naturalist. In 1835, his trip famously took him to the Galápagos Islands, a group of 19 Pacific islands located about 1,000 km west of Ecuador. He stayed there for five weeks.

2　During his time on the islands, Darwin studied and collected plants, animals and rock samples. After returning to London, he conducted detailed studies of the collection, and found that all of the species living on the Galápagos were native to the islands and were not found anywhere else in the world. All of them, however, closely resembled the species found on the South American mainland. This understanding made him speculate that, after arriving from the mainland, they slowly adapted to the environments of the islands and evolved into different species.

3　Darwin also noticed that there was a lot of competition among individual members of a single species. This made him think that, for example, a bird with a sharper beak than other birds in the local population might have a better chance of surviving and reproducing. Furthermore, if that characteristic were passed on to their offspring, those birds would dominate future populations, and the other birds would eventually disappear. Darwin called this process survival of the fittest, or natural selection.

4　Darwin worked on his theory of evolution through natural selection for more than 20 years before publishing it in his book *On the Origin of Species* in 1859. The book was widely accepted by the scientific community. Today, it is considered to be one of the most important academic books ever written.

> **Words:** naturalist 博物学者　species （生物の）種　adapted 適応した　evolved 進化した　beak くちばし
> reproducing 繁殖　passed on 受け継がれた　natural selection 自然選択　theory of evolution 進化論
> *On the Origin of Species* 『種の起源』

A Vocabulary Builder

次の単語の本文中での意味を、a. ～ c. の中から 1 つずつ選びましょう。

1. resembled (line 10):   a. followed   b. looked like   c. watched

2. speculate (line 11):   a. calculate   b. admit   c. think

3. evolved (line 13):   a. moved   b. developed   c. disappeared

4. offspring (line 17):   a. babies   b. bodies   c. parents

B Comprehension Questions

完成した英文が本文の内容に合うように、a. ～ c. の中から最も適切なものを 1 つずつ選びましょう。

1. The Galápagos are in the (a. Atlantic   b. Indian   c. Pacific) Ocean.

2. Darwin learned that all of the animal and plant species on the Galápagos were
   (a. unique to the area   b. found on the mainland   c. slowly disappearing).

3. The idea of natural selection came to Darwin after seeing (a. cooperation
   b. competition   c. communication) among members of a single species.

4. Darwin's book On the Origin of Species (a. was positively received   b. was negatively
   received   c. received little attention) in scientific circles.

C Paragraph Summaries

次の英文が表している本文の段落番号を（　）に記入しましょう。

(   ) Darwin made a five-year voyage that included a five-week stay on the Galápagos
        Islands.

(   ) Darwin's book describing his theory of evolution has become one of the most
        important books in history.

(   ) After careful study of the plants and animals found on the islands, Darwin came to
        think that they had all evolved into different species.

(   ) Darwin believed that living things which best adjusted to their environment would
        be the most successful in surviving and reproducing.

Listening

L の発音を意識して聞こう

L の発音には、「明るい L」と「暗い L」があります。light の L は明るい L ですが、これは舌先を歯茎に付けたまま発音します。暗い L の例は apple（/æpl/）で、「アポー」のように、こもった「オ」のように聞こえます。

Task ── 下線部が明るい L か暗い L かを意識しながら、リピートしましょう。──

1. I only know a few people in London.
2. His latest novel is about a girl who loves dolls.
3. Please dry the plates and glasses with this clean dish towel.

A 会話を聞き、下のイラストの内容が出てくる順番に 1 ～ 4 の番号を（ ）に記入しましょう。

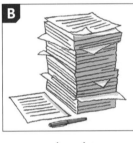

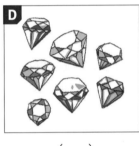

（　　　）　　　　　（　　　）　　　　　（　　　）　　　　　（　　　）

B もう一度会話を聞き、（ ）に単語を記入しましょう。

A: Did you have a favorite book when you were ¹(　　　　　)?

B: Well, I read all ²(　　　　　) the Harry Potter books by J.K. Rowling.

A: Really? Me too! You know, she started writing at a very young ³(　　　　　). And she wrote her first ⁴(　　　　　) when she was only eleven years old. It was about seven cursed* ⁵(　　　　).

B: I heard she got the idea for Harry Potter on a train from Manchester to London when she was about 25. And she wrote almost everything ⁶(　　　　) ⁷(　　　　)!

*cursed 呪われた

C 質問を聞き、最も適切な答えを a. ～ c. の中から 1 つずつ選びましょう。

1. a. b. c.　　　**2.** a. b. c.　　　**3.** a. b. c.　　　**4.** a. b. c.

84

Speaking

相づちを効果的に打って会話をしよう

相づちは会話の潤滑油です。気持ちや場面に応じて、さまざまな相づちの表現を使いこなしましょう。以下は会話で使える主な表現です。

> Really? [Seriously?]「本当？」、That's interesting [amazing/great]!「面白い（すごい／素晴らしい）ですね！」、I see.「なるほど」、Right.「そうですね」、Oh, yeah?「そうなの？」、Wow!「そうなの！」、No way!「信じられない！」、Uh-huh.（「うんうん」に相当）

Ex.

A: I saw the fashion model you were talking about the other day at the mall.

B: **Seriously?** How did she look?

A: She was much taller than I thought, and she looked absolutely brilliant.

B: **Uh-huh.** Anything else?

A: Oh, she was with a good-looking man. I'm sure they were dating!

B: **No way!** I don't want to believe that!

A 相づちの表現を 2 つ使って次の会話を完成させましょう。完成後、ペアで練習しましょう。

A: Who's your favorite entertainer or sportsperson?

B: Umm… _____.

A: _____. Why do you like _____?

B: Well, _____ and _____.

A: _____. Do you have any other reasons?

B: Yes, _____.

B 次の質問について、パートナーと会話をしましょう。

* historical figure 歴史上の人物

	Me	My Partner
1. Who was an important historical figure* in your country? Why?		
2. Who is an important person in your country today? Why?		

Writing

人物について説明する英文を書こう

人物について説明する英文を書く際は、以下のような流れで構成すると良いでしょう。以下の例文を読みながら、英文がどのように構成されているかを確認しましょう。

| ① 自分との関係 | ➡ | ② 理由1 | ➡ | ③ 理由2 | ➡ | ④ その人が与えた影響 |

Ex.

An important person in my life was my high school English teacher, Ms. Yamada.《自分との関係》 Her English class was always full of interesting activities.《理由1》 I was not good at English then, but she never gave up on me, and she helped me a lot.《理由2》 Thanks to her, I came to like English, and now I am majoring in English at university.《その人が与えた影響》

POINT 理由に具体的なエピソードを入れると説得力が増します。

Task 自分の人生に影響を与えた／与えている人物についてのパラグラフを書きましょう。

Step 1 以下のフレームを使ってアウトラインを作りましょう。

自分との関係 (relationship)	
理由1 (reason1)	
理由2 (reason2)	
その人が与えた影響 (impact)	

Step 2 Step 1のアウトラインをもとにパラグラフを書きましょう。

An important person in my life _____

_____

_____

_____ .

Unit 14

Food and Health

衣食住の中で、食は多くの人々にとって最も大きな興味・関心の的です。2013年には、「和食；日本人の伝統的な食文化」がユネスコ無形文化遺産に登録されるなど、日本を含め世界の国々にはさまざまな食文化があります。この Unit では、食について英語で理解したり表現したりする練習をしましょう。

Warm-Up Questions

次の質問に英語で答えましょう。

1. What are your favorite foods? How often do you eat them?

   _____

   _____

2. Do you think you are eating a healthy diet? Why or why not?

   _____

   _____

Reading

修飾関係に注目して英文を読もう

英語は、名詞に対して後ろから情報を追加する「後置修飾」が多く見られる言語です。英文を読む際は、名詞の後に来る関係詞（省略されて S+V が続く場合もある）や分詞などに注目して意味を取りましょう。

Superfoods

[1] Superfoods are nutrient-rich foods that are considered to be particularly beneficial to one's health. They can help us live longer and healthier lives, stay active and

5▶ improve our overall well-being. Most superfoods are plant-based, but some are animal-based as well. Blueberries, broccoli, avocados, soybeans, almonds, salmon and yogurt are just a few examples of foods that have been given the "superfood" label.

[2] Superfoods supply the body with large quantities of vitamins and minerals. The
10▶ high vitamin and mineral content found in superfoods can help the body fight off diseases and keep it healthy and strong. These nutrients also promote heart health, control weight, improve energy levels and even slow down the aging process.

[3] Additionally, superfoods provide the body with large amounts of antioxidants and phytochemicals. Antioxidants are substances that can prevent or slow damage to cells.
15▶ They may also help prevent cancer. Phytochemicals are the chemicals in plants that give them their flavor, color and aroma. Although phytochemicals have no nutritional value, it is believed that they help reduce the risk of cancer and heart disease, as well as improve the function of the immune system.

[4] While superfoods themselves may be healthful, their processing may not. For
20▶ example, many kinds of "super juices" actually contain large quantities of added sugar. Bottled green teas sold in some countries may also include sugar. Therefore, consumers should carefully read the label in order to make sure that the product they are buying is truly a superfood and not merely a product disguised as one.

Words: nutrient-rich 栄養価の高い　minerals ミネラル　antioxidants 抗酸化物質　phytochemicals 植物性化学物質　cells 細胞　cancer 癌　immune system 免疫システム　disguised 装った

A | Vocabulary Builder

次の単語の本文中での意味を、a. ～ c. の中から 1 つずつ選びましょう。

1. beneficial (line 2): **a.** harmless **b.** threatening **c.** useful

2. promote (line 11): **a.** assist with **b.** interact with **c.** interfere with

3. substances (line 14): **a.** cures **b.** vitamins **c.** materials

4. merely (line 23): **a.** greatly **b.** simply **c.** completely

B | Comprehension Questions

完成した英文が本文の内容に合うように、a. ～ c. の中から最も適切なものを 1 つずつ選びましょう。

1. (**a.** The majority of **b.** Less than half of **c.** No) superfoods come from animals.

2. The vitamins and minerals in superfoods (**a.** cause people to age faster **b.** slow the growing process **c.** provide energy to the body).

3. (**a.** Antioxidants have no **b.** Phytochemicals have no **c.** Neither antioxidants nor phytochemicals have any) nutritional content.

4. To ensure that a product is in fact a superfood, consumers are advised to (**a.** check the product label **b.** visit the company homepage **c.** consult with a store clerk).

C | Paragraph Summaries

次の英文が表している本文の段落番号を（ ）に記入しましょう。

( ) Superfoods contain high concentrations of vitamins and minerals that, among other things, help prevent diseases and keep the body strong.

( ) The processing of superfoods may produce some unhealthful results.

( ) Superfoods are foods rich in nutrients and considered to be very healthful.

( ) Antioxidants prevent or reduce cell damage, while phytochemicals fight certain diseases and boost the immune system.

Listening

二重母音に注意して聞こう

英語には、table の /eɪ/ や boat の /oʊ/ のように 2 つの母音が連続する二重母音があります。「テーブル」や「ボート」のように音を伸ばさず、「テイボォ」や「ボウトゥ」のように 2 つの母音を発音しましょう。

Task ──下線部の発音に注意して英文を聞き、リピートしましょう。──

1. It takes only a few minutes to get to the station. /oʊ/, /eɪ/

2. Most students were late for class this morning. /oʊ/, /eɪ/

3. Both the main actor and the director were on the stage. /oʊ/, /eɪ/

A 会話を聞き、下のイラストの内容が出てくる順番に 1 ～ 4 の番号を（　）に記入しましょう。

（　　）

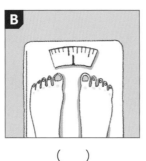
（　　）

（　　）

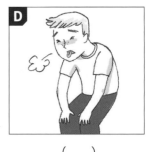
（　　）

B もう一度会話を聞き、（　）に単語を記入しましょう。

A: Hi, Bill. What seems to be the problem?

B: Well, doctor, I don't seem to have much energy these days. I get tired just walking to the
¹(　　　　　　), and I can't seem to ²(　　　　) asleep at night.

A: OK, let's check your ³(　　　　　). Could you step on the scale? … I see you've
⁴(　　　) a few kilos since your last visit. Are you eating a healthy diet?

B: No. Since I started living alone, I've been eating ⁵(　　　　) junk food.

A: You need to eat more nutritious food and ⁶(　　　　) more. If you do that, your
energy level will ⁷(　　　　), and you should be able to sleep more soundly.

C 質問を聞き、最も適切な答えを a. ～ c. の中から 1 つずつ選びましょう。

1. a. b. c.　　　**2.** a. b. c.　　　**3.** a. b. c.　　　**4.** a. b. c.

Speaking

《依頼》の表現を使って会話をしよう

相手に「～してください」と依頼をする場合、以下のような表現を使うことができます。

> Can [Will/Could/Would] you ...? / Please ... [..., please.] / Is it possible for you to ...? /
> Do you mind *doing*?

Ex.

B 71

A: Yesterday, I went to a restaurant that serves vegan dishes.

B: Vegan? **Can you** explain what that is?

A: A vegan is a person who doesn't eat any animal products such as meat, fish and eggs.

B: Oh, I see.

A: If you're interested, I can take you to the restaurant sometime.

B: That would be great! **Please let** me know when you're planning to go next.

A 依頼の表現を2つ使って次の会話を完成させましょう。完成後、ペアで練習しましょう。

A: Kim, we're going out for *shabu shabu* tonight. Do you want to come?

B: Umm…yes. But first, _____?

A: Sure. *Shabu shabu* is a kind of *nabe ryori*, or hot pot.

B: It sounds interesting. _____?

A: It contains things like _____.

B 次の質問について、パートナーと会話をしましょう。

	Me	My Partner
1. What did you have for breakfast, lunch and dinner yesterday?		
2. What are your three favorite vegetables?		
3. What are two healthy foods that you don't really like?		
4. How long do you exercise each day (including walking and cycling)?		

Writing

《情報の追加》を表す表現を使って英文を書こう

自分の述べたことに対して「そして」「さらに」「その上」といったように情報を追加したい場合は、以下のような表現を使うことができます。

in addition (to)　additionally　moreover　furthermore　also　besides　what is more

Ex.

As most of you know, natto is one of the healthiest foods. It is said to be effective in preventing arteriosclerosis*. **In addition**, natto is full of isoflavones*, which help keep our skin in good condition. **What is more**, natto contains a lot of vitamins B2 and K and calcium. You can find a lot of natto recipes on cooking websites, so please try some!

* arteriosclerosis 動脈硬化症　isoflavones イソフラボン

Task 健康的な生活の送り方についてのパラグラフを書きましょう。

Step 1 健康な生活を送るために心がけるべきことを3つ挙げましょう。

Ex) *Try not to eat between meals, especially junk food.*

Step 2 Step 1 のアウトラインをもとにパラグラフを書きましょう。

There are many things we can do in order to live a healthy life. For example, we should try not to eat between meals, especially junk food. In addition, _____ _____, _____ _____. And finally, _____ .

Unit 15

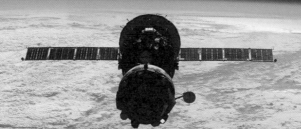

Space Exploration

1969 年に人類が初めて月面着陸を成功させて以来約半世紀が過ぎましたが、宇宙は依然として私たちに夢とロマンを与える空間です。その一方、科学技術の発展によって宇宙の謎は少しずつ解明されており、宇宙旅行もあながち夢物語ではなくなってきています。この Unit では、宇宙や宇宙探査について英語で理解したり表現したりする練習をしましょう。

Warm-Up Questions

宇宙に関するクイズに挑戦しましょう。

* Jupiter 木星　Mars 火星　Venus 金星

1. What is the temperature of the Sun?
   a. About 800°C　　　　b. About 2,000°C　　　　c. About 6,000°C

2. How far is it from the Earth to the Moon?
   a. 380,000 km　　　　b. 540,000 km　　　　c. 760,000 km

3. What is Jupiter* mostly made of?　　　a. ice　　b. gas　　c. rock

4. How long does it take for the light from the Sun to reach the Earth?
   a. 30s　　　　b. 5m48s　　　　c. 8m19s

5. Which is the largest planet, Mars*, Earth or Venus*?　a. Mars　b. Earth　c. Venus

Reading

意味のかたまり（チャンク）単位で内容を読み取ろう

意味のかたまり（チャンク）単位で意味を取っていくとスムーズに読み進めることができます。句や節の句切れを意識し、カンマや接続詞（and や but など）に注目して読みましょう。

Hayabusa2

1　In December, 2020, the space explorer Hayabusa2 returned to Earth and dropped a capsule containing soil samples from Ryugu, an asteroid located 300 million kilometers away. The probe
5 ▸ was launched on a rocket on November 30, 2014 and reached the one-kilometer long asteroid on July 27, 2018. After landing, the probe observed Ryugu for six months and took surface soil samples. A projectile was later fired into the rock, and a second probe gathered a sample of subsurface material.

2　The second sample has people in the scientific community very excited. It is the first
10 ▸ subsurface asteroid soil ever collected, and, contrary to the first sample, it is believed to have avoided contamination as Ryugu traveled the solar system. Scientists are hopeful that the soil will help explain how Earth was formed, and perhaps provide us with an understanding of where our organic materials originated.

3　Unlike planets, which have gradually transformed into increasingly complex
15 ▸ systems over their 4.6 billion years of existence, asteroids have remained unchanged and well preserved. That's why scientists think the asteroid may help us get a picture of what Earth looked like in its early stages of development. Hopes were further raised when it was confirmed in June of 2021 that one of the samples from Ryugu contained a large amount of hydrogen and organic matter.

20 ▸ 4　Since delivering the soil samples from Ryugu, the space explorer has continued on its journey, this time towards a ball-shaped asteroid called 199KY26. The asteroid is about 30 meters in diameter and rotates once every 10 minutes. Hayabusa2 is expected to reach the asteroid in July, 2031 and observe it by camera, but without landing on it.

Words: asteroid 小惑星　probe 探査機　projectile 発射体　contamination 汚染　solar system 太陽系
organic 有機的な　diameter 直径

94

A Vocabulary Builder

次の単語の本文中での意味を、a. ～ c. の中から 1 つずつ選びましょう。

1. capsule (line 2):   a. bomb   b. rocket   c. case

2. launched (line 5):   a. shot up   b. backed up   c. blown up

3. subsurface (line 10): a. exterior   b. underground   c. loose

4. preserved (line 16): a. accepted   b. organized   c. protected

B Comprehension Questions

完成した英文が本文の内容に合うように、a. ～ c. の中から最も適切なものを 1 つずつ選びましょう。

1. The second sample taken from Ryugu was made possible by (**a.** drilling a hole in the rock   **b.** shooting an object into the rock   **c.** freezing the rock).

2. (**a.** The surface   **b.** The subsurface   **c.** Neither) sample is believed to be contaminated.

3. Ryugu (**a.** probably doesn't contain organic material   **b.** has undergone many changes during its existence   **c.** has remained the same over the years).

4. Hayabusa2 is expected to (**a.** land on   **b.** take visual images of   **c.** collect soil samples from) asteroid 199KY26 in 2031.

C Paragraph Summaries

次の英文が表している本文の段落番号を（　）に記入しましょう。

(　　)   Large quantities of hydrogen and organic matter were found in one of the soil samples in June, 2021.

(　　)   In December 2020, Hayabusa2 returned to Earth following a six-year space journey, bringing with it two soil samples from a distant asteroid.

(　　)   Hayabusa2 is scheduled to reach a second asteroid in 2031.

(　　)   The second soil sample may give scientists clues about how Earth was born and where its organic matter came from.

Listening

子音が連続する音を意識して聞こう

英語には、例えば spl ash のように、母音に対して複数の子音が付く単語が多くあります。su・pu・ra・sshu のように余計な母音は入りませんので、注意して聞きましょう。

Task ——下線部の発音に注意して英文を聞き、リピートしましょう。——

1. The children enjoyed <u>spl</u>ashing around in the water.

2. <u>Pl</u>ease <u>pr</u>ess this button if you want to <u>pr</u>int the files.

3. I <u>tr</u>ied to find a <u>fl</u>ower shop along the <u>str</u>eet.

 会話を聞き、下のイラストの内容が出てくる順番に 1 〜 4 の番号を（　）に記入しましょう。

 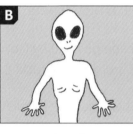 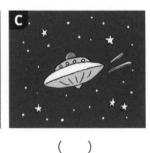 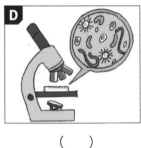

（　　）　　　　　　（　　）　　　　　　（　　）　　　　　　（　　）

 もう一度会話を聞き、（　）に単語を記入しましょう。

A: Do you believe ¹(　　　　　　) UFOs, Peter?

B: Unidentified ²(　　　　　) ³(　　　　　　　)? … No, I don't think so.

A: Then, do you think ⁴(　　　　　) life on other planets?

B: Little green men like E.T.? … No, but there ⁵(　　　　　) be microorganisms*.

A: If microorganisms exist on some planets, then don't you think there could be more advanced life ⁶(　　　　) on others—even more advanced than us?

B: Maybe. But if that were ⁷(　　　　　　), I think they would have found us by now.

A: Maybe they already have. …

*microorganism 微生物

 質問を聞き、最も適切な答えを a. 〜 c. の中から 1 つずつ選びましょう。

1. a. b. c.　　　2. a. b. c.　　　3. a. b. c.　　　4. a. b. c.

Unit **15** **Space Exploration**

Speaking

Yes か No で答え切れない質問に対応しよう

会話の中で、Yes か No か答え切れない質問を受けることがあります。そのときは、Yes and no.（はいでもあり、いいえでもあります）や It depends.（場合によります）、It's hard to say（答えるのが難しいです）といった表現が使えます。また、That's a hard [difficult] question (to answer) という表現を出だしに使うと良いでしょう。

Ex.

A: Sorry to ask you such a strange question, but do you believe in aliens?

B: **That's a hard question to answer**, but I would say **yes and no**. I believe there are some kinds of living creatures out there, but not like the aliens we see in typical SF movies. What do you think?

A: Just like you, I would say **it depends**. I don't think there are any human-like aliens out there, but there might be some other kinds of life forms.

A 上で挙げた表現を 2 つ使って次の会話を完成させましょう。完成後、ペアで練習しましょう。

A: Do you think space vacations will be popular in the future?

B: _____.

A: If you won a free ticket for a trip in space, would you go?

B: _____.

A: OK, one more question. Is space exploration important? Why or why not?

B: _____.

B 次の質問について、パートナーと会話をしましょう。

	Me	My Partner
1. Do you believe in UFOs? Why or why not?		
2. What do you think you would do if you saw a UFO land and aliens started walking towards you?		
3. Would you like to be an astronaut? Why or why not?		

97

Writing

問題発見・解決型の英文を書こう

問題発見・解決型の文章はこれからの時代において多く求められる文章のタイプです。基本的には以下の流れに沿って文章を構成すると良いでしょう。

何が問題なのか ➡ 問題の追加説明 ➡ 対策 ➡ 課題

Ex.

Space debris* refers to human-made objects that are moving around Earth but are no longer used. (何が問題なのか) As space debris moves at an extremely fast speed, it can cause serious damage to satellites and spacecraft when it crashes into them. (問題の追加説明) One way to remove it is to use laser beams to either destroy it or change its direction. (対策) However, the effect is very limited because the amount of debris is so large. (課題) * space debris /dəbríː/ 宇宙ゴミ

POINT 紙幅に余裕があれば、問題の追加説明や対策を膨らませると説得力が増します。

Task 宇宙飛行士が宇宙生活で直面する問題についてのパラグラフを書きましょう。

Step 1 宇宙飛行士が宇宙生活で直面する問題を以下の中から 2 つ選び、どのように対応しているのかを調べてまとめましょう。

sleeping / taking a bath / exercising / cooking

Problem（問題）	Solution（解決策）

Step 2 Step 1 のアウトラインをもとにパラグラフを書きましょう。

I'd like to discuss two problems that astronauts face when in space, and their solutions. First is the problem of _____. To solve this problem, _____

_____

_____

_____

クラス用音声CD有り（別売）

English In Tune

ストラテジー別に学ぶ4技能融合型テキスト

2022年2月1日　初版発行
2023年2月10日　第 2 刷

著　者　Robert Hickling / 森本 俊
発行者　松村達生
発行所　センゲージ ラーニング株式会社
　　　　〒102-0073　東京都千代田区九段北1-11-11　第2フナトビル5階
　　　　電話 03-3511-4392
　　　　FAX 03-3511-4391
　　　　e-mail: eltjapan@cengage.com
　　　　copyright © 2022 センゲージ ラーニング株式会社

装丁・組版　　藤原志麻（クリエイド・ラーニング株式会社）
編集協力　　　クリエイド・ラーニング株式会社
本文イラスト　Nozomi Inoue
印刷・製本　　株式会社エデュプレス

ISBN 978-4-86312-393-9